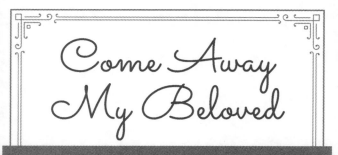

# Come Away My Beloved

## 3-MINUTE DEVOTIONS FOR WOMEN

D1517016

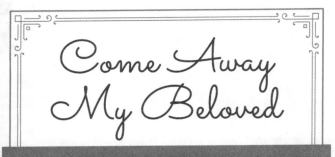

# Come Away My Beloved

## 3-MINUTE DEVOTIONS FOR WOMEN

FRANCES J. ROBERTS

**BARBOUR BOOKS**
An Imprint of Barbour Publishing, Inc.

© 2020 by Frances J. Roberts

Compiled and edited by Shanna D. Gregor

Print ISBN 978-1-64352-250-0

eBook Editions:
Adobe Digital Edition (.epub) 978-1-64352-559-4
Kindle and MobiPocket Edition (.prc) 978-1-64352-560-0

Published by Barbour Books, an imprint of Barbour Publishing, Inc., 1810 Barbour Drive, Uhrichsville, Ohio 44683, www.barbourbooks.com

*Our mission is to inspire the world with the life-changing message of the Bible.*

Member of the
Evangelical Christian
Publishers Association

Printed in the United States of America.

## Introduction

This special 3-Minute Devotions edition of *Come Away My Beloved* marks and celebrates the 50th anniversary of Frances J. Roberts's best-selling devotional that has touched millions of lives in its half century. Readers have found peace, challenge, encouragement, and comfort in page after page of biblical insight from the author's pen and heart.

This edition takes Frances's original, classic devotional, edited and presented in 180 bite-size readings (including her poetry and prayers) that can be read in 3 minutes (or less). Some additional scripture has been included in this edition as well.

Be blessed!
The Publisher

# Preface

*Come Away My Beloved* was forged in the crucible of life. In the midst of each day's joys and trials has come the ministering spirit of the Heavenly Father and the Lord Jesus Christ, bringing words of encouragement, hope, comfort, and conviction.

To gain the maximum blessing from this book, read it carefully and prayerfully, a little at a time, searching always for the special treasure of truth for your own need. He who knows you by name and understands your deepest longings will speak to your heart from these pages, shutting out the world about you and bringing you into fellowship with Himself.

Whether you are just beginning your Christian walk or have grown into a fuller stature in Christ, you will be equally challenged and helped. Some books give instruction for Christian living; others inspire to greater devotion. *Come Away My Beloved* will do both as you open your soul to its living message.

With this book go many prayers that God

will enrich every life it touches. Surely, we are all bound together in one family in Christ through the bonds of His Holy Spirit.

FJR

# The Call of Love

*My beloved spake, and said unto me, Rise up,*
*my love, my fair one, and come away.*

SONG OF SOLOMON 2:10

O My beloved, abide under the shelter of the lattice—for I have betrothed thee unto Myself, and though ye are sometimes indifferent toward Me, My love for thee is at all times as a flame of fire. My ardor never cools. My longing for thy love and affection is deep and constant.

Tarry not for an opportunity to have more time to be alone with Me. Take it, though ye leave the tasks at hand. Nothing will suffer. Things are of less importance than ye think. Our time together is like a garden full of flowers, whereas the time ye give to things is as a field full of stubble.

# The Call of Love

## PART 2

*There is no fear in love; but perfect love casteth out fear: because fear hath torment. He that feareth is not made perfect in love.*

1 JOHN 4:18

I love thee, and if ye can always, as it were, feel My pulsebeat, ye shall know many things the knowledge of which shall give thee sustaining strength. I bare thy sins and I wish to carry thy burdens. Ye may have the gift of a light and merry heart. My love bower is the place where ye shall find it, for My love dispels all fear and is a cure for every ill. Lay thy head upon My breast and lose thyself in Me. Thou shalt experience resurrection life and peace; the joy of the Lord shall become thy strength; and wells of salvation shall be opened within thee.

# The Need for Greater Faith

*When Jesus heard it, he marvelled, and said
to them that followed, Verily I say unto you,
I have not found so great faith, no, not in Israel.*

MATTHEW 8:10

O My child, do not expect the trials to be lighter than in the past. Why should ye think the testings would be less severe? Lo, I prove all things, and there are areas of thy life that I have not touched as yet. Do not look for respite. The days ahead may call for greater endurance and more robust faith than ye have ever needed before. Welcome this, for ye must surely know by this time how precious are the lessons learned through such experiences. If it is not fully possible to anticipate them with joy, it is certainly not difficult to gain an appropriate appreciation of them afterward, in retrospect.

# Resignation

*Trust in the LORD with all thine heart; and lean not unto thine own understanding.*

PROVERBS 3:5

Incline thine heart unto Me, and let thine ear be attuned to My voice. For lo, I would speak to thee, and I have an urgent message to give thee.

Go not about to establish thine own designs. Lo, I have already set in motion My divine will and purpose and I would not have thee interfere. I am jealous about My children: Lo, they are Mine, saith the Lord; and ye shall not intrude in any way such as would hinder My plans from working out. Yea, ye may do many things, but only that which I direct thee to do can have My blessing upon it.

# Resignation
## PART 2

*Be careful for nothing; but in every thing by
prayer and supplication with thanksgiving
let your requests be made known unto God.
And the peace of God, which passeth all
understanding, shall keep your hearts
and minds through Christ Jesus.*

PHILIPPIANS 4:6-7

Resign all into My hands—thy loved ones as
well as thine own self. Be obedient to the still
small voice. Thine own imaginings may speak
more loudly, but wait upon Me always. Ye shall
see the wisdom and the glory in this in due time.
Fret not about carnal things, but concern thyself
first and always about spiritual values. Truly,
My promise is still: "Seek ye first the Kingdom
of God, and all the other needful things shall be
added unto thee."

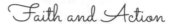

# Faith and Action

*And they were helped against them, and the
Hagarites were delivered into their hand, and
all that were with them: for they cried to God
in the battle, and he was intreated of them;
because they put their trust in him.*

1 CHRONICLES 5:20

My promises are of no avail to thee except
as ye apply and appropriate them by faith. In
thy daily walk, ye shall be victorious only to the
degree that ye trust Me. I can help thee only as ye
ask. I shall meet you at every point where ye put
action alongside thy prayers. Only as ye WALK
shall the waters of adversity be parted before
thee. Overburdened as the world is with trouble
and sickness, I need those who have proved My
sufficiency in everyday, personal experience to
lead the suffering to the fountains of life.

# Faith and Action
## PART 2

*Therefore if thine enemy hunger, feed him;*
*if he thirst, give him drink: for in so doing thou*
*shalt heap coals of fire on his head. Be not*
*overcome of evil, but overcome evil with good.*

ROMANS 12:20–21

*I need those* who have found Me as burden-bearer to help bring deliverance to the oppressed. Never begrudge time given to chronic complainers, but recognize in each encounter the opportunity to speak a word that may lead to their liberation. No case is too hard for Me. Never be taken by surprise when I use you to change a pattern. Do not judge a man by what he appears to be, but see him as what he CAN be if he gives himself unreservedly to Me.

# Sincerity

*Jesus answered and said unto him, Verily,*
*verily, I say unto thee, Except a man be born*
*again, he cannot see the kingdom of God.*

JOHN 3:3

Marvel not that I have said that ye must be born anew. Of the flesh, nothing that is spiritual can ever be produced. Spiritual life shall bring forth that which is spiritual; and likewise, carnal flesh shall bring forth only more carnality.

This is why I said I loathed your sacrifices. It was not that I despised the ordinance in itself, but that I perceived that it was a product of the flesh—an expression of self-righteousness and indifference to the claim of God upon thy heart.

My ordinances are good and holy, but they are to be entered into with deep sincerity and with awareness of their true significance. To sacrifice in carelessness and ignorance is to damage thine own soul. Let thy spirit never become callous.

# Sincerity
## PART 2

*But the natural man receiveth not the things
of the Spirit of God: for they are foolishness
unto him: neither can he know them, because
they are spiritually discerned.*

1 CORINTHIANS 2:14

Without holiness, no man shall see God. This could be as truly stated, "Without a tender heart and sensitive, attentive spirit, none shall see God," for without these, no true holiness will ever be attained.

The fool shall not discern the value and shall cast aside great treasure. The practiced eye knoweth the true worth of a gem and shall not let it escape him. Thus shall ye be in spiritual matters.

Train thine eye to discern that which is of true worth, and let it not escape thee.

# Guidance

*I will guide thee with mine eye.*

PSALM 32:8

My child, hear My voice, and give no heed to the voice of the stranger. My paths are straight, and they are narrow, but ye shall have no difficulty in finding them if ye watch Me. I am guiding thee. Ye need not look to man for direction. Ye may learn much by fellowship with the saints, but never allow any to take the part that is rightfully Mine—to direct thy steps. As it is written, "The steps of a good man are ORDERED BY THE LORD"—not by the preacher, not by some Christian worker, but by the Lord.

Trust Me to do it, and give Me the time and the opportunity to do it. Be not hasty, and lean not upon thine own intelligence.

Rest in Me. I shall bring to pass My perfect will in thy life as ye believe and live in faith.

# On the Waters of Sorrow

*And he said, Come. And when*
*Peter was come down out of the ship,*
*he walked on the water, to go to Jesus.*

MATTHEW 14:29

O My child, I am coming to thee walking upon the waters of the sorrows of thy life; yea, above the sounds of the storm ye shall hear My voice calling thy name.

Ye are never alone, for I am at thy right hand. Never despair, for I am watching over and caring for thee. Be NOT anxious. What seemeth to thee to be at present a difficult situation is all part of My planning, and I am working out the details of circumstances to the end that I may bless thee and reveal Myself to thee in a new way.

# On the Waters of Sorrow
## PART 2

*And the LORD spake unto Moses face to face,*
*as a man speaketh unto his friend.*

EXODUS 33:11

As I have opened thine eyes to see, so shall I open thine ears to hear, and ye shall come to know Me even as did Moses, yea, in a face-to-face relationship.

For I shall remove the veil that separates Me from thee, and ye shall know Me as thy dearest Friend and as thy truest Comforter.

No darkness shall hide the shining of My face, for I shall be to thee as a bright star in the night sky. Never let thy faith waver. Reach out thy hand, and thou shalt touch the hem of My garment.

# Set Thy Course by My Promises

*Now to Abraham and his seed*
*were the promises made. He saith not,*
*And to seeds, as of many; but as of one,*
*And to thy seed, which is Christ.*

GALATIANS 3:16

Hold to My promises. They are given to thee as a chart is given to a ship, and a compass to the hunter. Ye may set thy course or find thy way by My promises. They will lead thee and guide thee in places where there is no trodden path. They will give thee direction and wisdom and will open up thine own understanding.

Study My Word, the Bible. Lo, it aboundeth with nuggets of courage. They will strengthen thee and help thee, and even in eternity ye shall partake of their far-reaching effects.

# Dependence on God

*And thine ears shall hear a word behind
thee, saying, This is the way, walk ye
in it, when ye turn to the right hand,
and when ye turn to the left.*

Isaiah 30:21

Ye cannot know what lieth in the distance, nor what adversity ye may encounter tomorrow. So walk closely with Me, that ye may be able to draw quickly upon My aid. Ye need Me; and no matter how well-developed is thy faith nor how mature is thy growth in grace, never think for a moment that ye need My support any less. Nay, but the truth is that ye need it even more. For I shelter the new-born from many a trial and testing such as I permit to confront those who are growing up in spiritual stature. Yea, verily, ye cannot grow unless I do bring into your lives these proving and testing experiences.

# Dependence on God
## PART 2

*I the LORD have called thee in righteousness,
and will hold thine hand, and will keep thee,
and give thee for a covenant of the people,
for a light of the Gentiles.*

ISAIAH 42:6

So hold thee more firmly to My hand as ye journey on in thy Christian walk. Trust not in thine own increasing strength; for verily, it is not thy strength but rather My strength within thee that ye feel. Ye are as vulnerable to the treachery of the enemy and as frail as ever; but thy knowledge of Me has deepened, and because of this thy trust in Me should come easier.

Move forward with courage and confidence; but always allow Me to walk ahead, and choose the right path for thee.

# The Burden Bearer

*For my yoke is easy, and my burden is light.*

MATTHEW 11:30

My child, do not share thy burdens with all who come unto thee professing concern. Lo, I, Myself, am the great burden-bearer. Ye need not look to another. I will lead thee and guide thee in wisdom from above. All things shall be as I plan them, if ye allow Me the freedom to shape circumstances and lead thee to the right decisions.

I am merciful and kind. I love thee beyond measure. I purpose to do thee good; and lo, I will bring unto thee those who can TRULY help, if ye leave all in My hands.

I want thee to prosper and be in health. I want thee to know Me more intimately. If difficulties come, it is by My order and for thy benefit. Man would say ye have trouble: I would say ye have a test.

# Safety in God's Will

*A man's heart deviseth his way:*
*but the Lord directeth his steps.*

PROVERBS 16:9

My will is not a place, but a condition. Do not ask Me WHERE and WHEN, but ask Me HOW? You will discover blessing in every place, and any place, if thy spirit is in tune with Me. No place nor time is more hallowed than another when ye are truly in love with Me.

I direct every motion of thy life, as the ocean bears a ship. Your will and intelligence may be at the helm, but divine providence and sovereignty are stronger forces. Ye can trust Me, knowing that any pressure I bring to bear upon thy life is initiated by My love, and I will not do even this except as ye are willing and desire.

## Safety in God's Will

### PART 2

*Whereas ye know not what shall be on
the morrow. For what is your life? It is
even a vapour, that appeareth for a
little time, and then vanisheth away.
For that ye ought to say, If the Lord will,
we shall live, and do this, or that.*

JAMES 4:14–15

Many a ship has sailed from port to port with no interference by Me, because Strong Will has been at the wheel. Multitudes of pleasure cruises go merrily in their ways, untouched by the power of My hand.

But ye have put thy life into My keeping, and because ye are depending on Me for guidance and direction, I shall give it.

Move on steadily, and know that the waters that carry thee are the waters of My love and My kindness, and I will keep thee on the right course.

# Release Thy Grief

*Surely he hath borne our griefs,*
*and carried our sorrows: yet we did esteem*
*him stricken, smitten of God, and afflicted.*
*But he was wounded for our transgressions,*
*he was bruised for our iniquities: the*
*chastisement of our peace was upon him;*
*and with his stripes we are healed.*

ISAIAH 53:4–5

My child, lean thy head upon My bosom. Well I know thy weariness, and every burden I would lift. Never bury thy griefs; but offer them up to Me. Thou wilt relieve thy soul of much strain if ye can lay every care in My hand. Never cling to any trouble, hoping to resolve it thyself, but turn it over to Me; and in doing so, ye shall free Me to work it out.

# Ministering Angels

*Are they not all ministering spirits,*
*sent forth to minister for them who*
*shall be heirs of salvation?*

HEBREWS 1:14

Surely He hath given thee ministering angels, and these may sometimes be in the form of thy friends. Accept their ministry as from God, and it shall be doubled in blessing. Ye may also, in turn, be used in similar manner to bless others.

Look not to the physical, alone, for the transmission of spiritual energy. Divine life can flow out to others through thy thoughts, the same as through thy hands. Use My power, and let it flow forth in any form I choose, as I direct and guide you. Ye may multiply thy ministry an hundredfold in this way. Be not restricted by thy present knowledge, but move in and learn more from Me.

# Walk On with Me

*I said in mine heart, God shall judge the*
*righteous and the wicked: for there is a time*
*there for every purpose and for every work.*

ECCLESIASTES 3:17

My child, the path of duty is before thee. It may look rugged, but it is the only way of divine blessing. Choose out some other way, and ye shall find only disappointment and frustration of soul. Weariness shall overtake thee on the smoothest road, if it be not the pathway of my ordained will.

Be not deceived by doubts, and be not detained by fears. Move into the center of My purposes for you: ye shall find there are glorious victories waiting for thee, and recompenses far exceeding every sacrifice.

# Walk On with Me

## PART 2

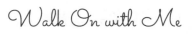

*That all the people of the earth may know
that the LORD is God, and that there is none
else. Let your heart therefore be perfect with
the LORD our God, to walk in his statutes, and
to keep his commandments, as at this day.*

1 KINGS 8:60–61

Be obedient: ye shall bring joy to My heart. Neither the applause nor the scorn of men should be of any consequence to thee. My approval is reward enough, and without this, any other satisfaction is not worthy of thy pursuit.

Walk on with Me. I shall be very near to give thee support and encouragement, so ye have nothing to warrant thy fears. They shall vanish as ye obey.

# The Vineyard of Prayer

*Praying always with all prayer
and supplication in the Spirit.*

EPHESIANS 6:18

O My child, the days are fraught with burdens that need to be borne upon the shoulders of faithful prayer warriors. Where are the ones who are willing to make themselves available to the Spirit for this ministry? Lo, I say, the Word sown shall dry up like carelessly strewn seed if it be not watered with tears of intercession. Ye cannot in yourself lay this ministry upon thy soul, but ye CAN make room in thy life for time apart with Me; and as ye place thyself at the disposal of the Holy Spirit, He shall use thee as a channel when the needs arise.

Nothing is more needful at this present hour than prayer power in full operation, under the direction and in the unction of the Holy Spirit.

# The Vineyard of Prayer
## PART 2

*Pray always.*

LUKE 21:36

I am calling My Spirit-filled believers to concerted and concentrated labor in this, the vineyard of prayer. Hidden from the eye of man, it is wide open to heaven; and the saints in heaven join with you in this operation of the love of God.

Other ministries ye must carry on yourselves alone, but in this ye have a mutual fellowship, for those in heaven have also an intercessory ministry for their brethren yet on earth.

Rejoice to be granted the privilege of so sacred a task. Count it most precious, and guard against the intrusion of distractions. Nothing is more important in My sight of all that ye can do for Me. Cherish it and cultivate it. Live in prayer, and ye shall know a full life of joy and the remuneration of My blessing!

# A Yielded, Believing Vessel

*And I sought for a man among them,*
*that should make up the hedge, and stand*
*in the gap before me for the land, that I*
*should not destroy it: but I found none.*

EZEKIEL 22:30

*I am never* in defeat, but I am held in abeyance at this present time by the selfishness and willfulness of man. Yea, the going forth of My justice and of My mercy is obstructed by the ignorance of men and by the lack of faith in even My children.

Be not dismayed and ill of heart and spirit. Hast thou not read how I could not do mighty works in their midst because of unbelief? It is no less true today—and it is not in one place but in many places—yea, even throughout the length and breadth of the land.

Be aware of Me. I can accomplish great things through even one yielded, believing vessel.

# Cherish My Words

*Thy word is a lamp unto my feet,*
*and a light unto my path.*

PSALM 119:105

O My children, obey My words. Do not wander in unbelief and darkness, but let the scripture shine as a light upon thy path. My Words shall be life unto thee, for My commandments are given for thy health and for any preservation. They will guard thee from folly, and guide thee away from danger.

Hide My commandments in thy heart, and make them the law of thy life. Cherish My words, and take not lightly the least of them. I have not given them to bind thee, but to bring thee into the life of greatest joy and truest liberty. . . .

Sanctification is accomplished in no one by accident. Learn My rules, and put them into practice consistently, if ye desire to see progress in the growth of thy soul.

# Comfort in Affliction

*The LORD is my rock, and my fortress,*
*and my deliverer; my God,*
*my strength, in whom I will trust.*

PSALM 18:2

O My people, hath not My hand wrought for thee with many signs and wonders? Have I not ministered unto thee in miraculous fashion? How sayest thou therefore in thine heart, "I will turn me again to the arm of flesh"? How oft have I spoken unto thee, and never failed to keep My word? Will ye not, then, trust Me now in this new emergency, even as ye have trusted Me in the past?

Thy need is deeper this time, and so I have made the testing more acute. I deepen you in the furnace of affliction, and purify your soul in the fires of pain.

Lean hard upon Me, for I bring thee through to new victories, and restoration shall follow what seemeth now to be a wind of destruction.

# Comfort in Affliction
## PART 2

*Ye are the light of the world. A city that is set on an hill cannot be hid.*

MATTHEW 5:14

Hold fast to My hand, and rest in My love, for of this ye may be very certain: My love is unaltered; yea, I have thee in My own INTENSIVE CARE. My concern for thee is deeper now than when things are normal.

Draw upon the resources of My grace, and so shall ye be equipped to communicate peace and confidence to thy dear ones. Heaven rejoices when ye go through trials with a singing spirit. Thy Father's heart is cheered when ye endure the test and question not His mercy.

Be as a beacon light. His own glorious radiance shall shine forth through thee, and Christ Himself shall be revealed.

# Return unto Me

*Therefore also now, saith the LORD,*
*turn ye even to me with all your heart,*
*and with fasting, and with weeping,*
*and with mourning.*

JOEL 2:12

Return unto Me; for lo, I have sought after thee, but thou hast continued on in pursuit of thine own ways. I have called unto thee, but ye have disregarded Me. I have placed obstacles in thy path, hoping that ye would stop and consider and inquire of Me, but ye have obstinately and determinately forged on ahead. . . .

Put down thine anxieties, and trust Me for everything. Ye need nothing but what I am fully able to supply, with no effort on thy part. I do not ask all My children to live in so complete a degree of trust, but I require it of THEE, because ye cannot please Me with anything less.

# Return to Me

## PART 2

*And rend your heart, and not your garments,
and turn unto the LORD your God: for he is
gracious and merciful, slow to anger, and of
great kindness, and repenteth him of the evil.*

JOEL 2:13

*Ye are weary,* and ye should be strong. Ye are encumbered, and I would have thee free. Ye are hindered by undue concerns, when ye should be abounding in joy.

Come back into My perfect will, and finish the task I have assigned thee. Anything else is sin. What for another may be legitimate is not so for thee.

Come close to Me, and I will minister to thee and will revive thy spirit. So shall ye go on, even though the climb be steeper than ever before.

# One Day at a Time

*Take therefore no thought for the morrow: for the morrow shall take thought for the things of itself.*

MATTHEW 6:34

O My child, hast thou known the way of the Lord, and canst thou trust Him now? Nothing shall befall thee but such as cometh from His hand. None shall set upon thee to hurt thee, for thy God hath built about thee a wall of fire.

Be content with what each day bringeth, rejoicing in thy God, for surely He it is who shall deliver thee and He it is who hath brought thee thither.

His way is discernable to the eye of faith. His heart is surely thy strong tower. In His affection thou hast security. In His love is thy hope and thy peace.

Do not question and do not doubt. Each day holdeth some small joy that shall escape thee if thou art preoccupied with tomorrow.

# One Day at a Time
## PART 2

*Then said Jesus to those Jews which
believed on him, If ye continue in my word,
then are ye my disciples indeed.*

JOHN 8:31

Nothing daunts thy Father. Nothing can restore the past and nothing can bind the future, but today thou mayest live in the full blessing of the Father's smile. Hold to His Words, for they are as a nail driven in a sure place. All else may seem shifting and non-permanent, but His Word is firm. It is a rock that shall not be moved. It is a firm place to stand.

Do not walk in the path of human reason, and resist the pressures that would project thee into conjectures of the future. Live one day at a time! Suffice it to keep thee occupied simply striving to bring joy to the Father's heart. For ye know that He loveth thee, and ye shall find thy peace.

# The Healing Power of Joy

*Now the God of hope fill you with all joy and peace in believing, that ye may abound in hope, through the power of the Holy Ghost.*

ROMANS 15:13

Praise Me. This I ask of thee in times when it seemeth indescribably difficult to do so. I ask it of thee in love that is stern at this point because I know unequivocally that it is your only hope for survival.

Distress of soul and grief of heart can only bring on destruction of body. Joy alone is a healer, and ye can have it in the darkest hour if ye will force thy soul to rise to Me in worship and adoration. I have not failed thee and ye have not failed Me. . . .

Let His peace flow in thee like a river, carrying away all the poison of painful memories and bringing to thee a fresh, clear stream of pure life and restoring thoughts.

# The Healing Power of Joy
## PART 2

*Restore unto me the joy of thy salvation;*
*and uphold me with thy free spirit.*

PSALM 51:12

*Bring thy sorrow,* and watch for the sunrise of the resurrection. Yea, verily there cometh always a resurrection—a morning when hope is reborn and life finds new beginning. Wait for it as tulip bulbs anticipate the spring. The rarest blooms are enhanced by the coldness of winter. The snow plays her part in producing the pageant of spring. But when the blossoms break through, we do not then turn back to thought of winter, but instead, we look ahead to the full joys of the coming summer.

So ye must do also. Thy God. . .is mighty to save. Yea, He is not only mighty to save from sin, but He is mighty to save from despair, from sorrow, from disappointment, from regret, from remorse, from self-castigation, and from the hot, blinding tears of rebellion against fateful circumstances.

# The Divine Commission

*And he said unto them, Go ye into
all the world, and preach the
gospel to every creature.*

MARK 16:15

The Saviour loves the dying world and the lost sinner no less today than He loved them the day He hung on Calvary, bleeding and dying for their redemption. . . . The preaching of the Gospel is still His will, and the salvation of souls is His chief concern. So also should it be thine, and nothing else should be permitted to take precedence over evangelism in thy life.

Be diligent. Confess thy lack, and repent of thy negligence. Then shall I give thee a fresh anointing and a new commission. Yea, I will give thee the tongue of an evangelist and will send thee forth to reap precious souls. Jesus, the Christ, shall be thy theme, and thou shalt uplift Him, and He shall draw the lost unto Himself.

# Eternity and Time

*And when these things begin to come to
pass, then look up, and lift up your heads;
for your redemption draweth nigh.*

LUKE 21:28

*Behold,* a *new* day is dawning! Let not the
sound of war and discord deafen thine ears to
My message; for I would speak to thee a word of
encouragement and would bring thee tidings of
hope.

I say unto thee, My little children, I have
not gone away never to return; but I shall surely
come, yea, even at a time when ye feel the least
expectation and when many shall have become
engrossed in the problems of the hour.

Lo, I say unto thee, My beloved ones, do not
become centered in the problems of the world;
but look up, for surely your deliverance is near.

# Eternity and Time
## PART 2

*And that, knowing the time, that now it is high time to awake out of sleep: for now is our salvation nearer than when we believed.*

ROMANS 13:11

My ageless purposes are set in Eternity. Time is as a little wheel set within the big wheel of Eternity. The little wheel turneth swiftly and shall one day cease. The big wheel turneth not, but goeth straight forward. Time is thy responsibility—Eternity is Mine! Ye shall move into thy place in the big wheel when the little wheel is left behind. See that now ye redeem the time, making use of it for the purposes of My eternal kingdom, thus investing it with something of the quality of the big wheel. . . .

Fill thy days with light and love and testimony. . . . So shall eternity inhabit thy heart and thou shalt deliver thy soul from the bondages of time.

# Eternity and Time
## PART 3

*There remaineth therefore
a rest to the people of God.*
HEBREWS 4:9

Thou shalt experience a liberation from the pressures of time and shalt in thine own heart slow down the little wheel. So shall ye find a new kind of rest. Ye shall have a foretaste of the Sabbath rest, into which the whole earth shall enter before long. When this time comes, I Myself will slow down the little wheel of time, and there shall be an adjustment, and it shall be as it was in the beginning.

. . .Ye have found the Spirit always unhurried, and ye have marvelled to find how oblivious ye had been to the passage of time whenever ye have been truly in the Spirit.

Ye can live here as much as ye choose. . . . Always it shall most certainly be a tremendous source of energy and vitality for thy spiritual life!

# He Hath Filled My Cup

*And he said unto me, It is done. I am Alpha
and Omega, the beginning and the end.*

REVELATION 21:6

He hath put a song in my mouth; He hath put
gladness in my heart. Yea, He is altogether lovely:
More than tongue can express or finite mind
can know. For He hath stretched forth His mighty
hand And hath smitten the waters: He hath made
me to pass through dry-shod. Hallelujah!

For there shall be no more sea (Rev. 21:1).

There shall be no more any separation!

He hath removed every barrier; He hath
bridged the gulf.

He hath drawn me unto Himself, yea, into
Himself.

He hath left the enemy in confusion and
defeat.

He hath led me through the way of the
wilderness,

And His hand hath been a shade from the
burning heat.

Through the barren wasteland, He hath filled
my cup from living streams.

# He Hath Filled My Cup
## PART 2

*He brought me up also out of an horrible pit...*
*and set my feet upon a rock.*

PSALM 40:2

He hath sustained, He hath delivered, He hath revealed Himself

In the cloud, in the fire, and in the Shekinah Glory. Lo, as if this had not been enough, He brought me to the banks of Jordan. There He did precede me: For as the priests went first, bearing the ark, So He did pass ahead in full possession of all His promises, And thus He opened my way and Brought me into the land that floweth with milk and honey (Joshua 3:16, 17; 4:24).

A land of promise, a land of fulfillment; A land of conquest, a land of victory. A land of fulness, a land of abundance; A land of fatness, a land of unreserved blessing.

Yea, He hath been unperturbed, though the inhabitants Of the land be giants: *For in His sight they be as grasshoppers!* And one with Him shall be mightier than them all.

# A Perpetual Fountain of Glory

*For the LORD thy God bringeth thee*
*into a good land, a land of brooks of*
*water, of fountains and depths that*
*spring out of valleys and hills.*

DEUTERONOMY 8:7

Look thou unto Me, and I will be unto thee as a beacon in the night, and thou shalt not stumble over the hidden thing. Yea, thou shalt walk in a way of victory though turmoil be on either hand, even as Israel marched through the Red Sea on a path which My hand hewed out for them. Yea, it shall be a path of deliverance, and My Spirit shall go with thee and thou shalt carry the glad tidings of deliverance to a people that sit in darkness and captivity.

Tarry thou not for a convenient time, . . . for My plan for thee excels all other ways, and in the center of My will there is a Perpetual Fountain of Glory.

# A Perpetual Fountain of Glory
## PART 2

*If ye then, being evil, know how to give good
gifts unto your children, how much more shall
your Father which is in heaven give good
things to them that ask him?*

MATTHEW 7:11

Doubt not, neither hesitate, for I the Lord thy God do go before thee, and thou hast already My promise that the work which I begin I am able to carry through to completion.

Yea, there is already laid up an exceeding weight of glory for those who go through with Me and determine to seize the prize. For I have wealth beyond thy fondest dreams to bestow upon them that have "left all to follow," and all the glittering enticements of this transient life are as chaff in comparison, for the gifts and calling of God are without repentance, and My giving is restricted only by the will and choice of the recipient.

# A Perpetual Fountain of Glory
## PART 3

*Stand fast therefore in the liberty wherewith
Christ hath made us free, and be not
entangled again with the yoke of bondage.*

### GALATIANS 5:1

Lord Jesus, I cast myself at Thy feet. Yea, let me bathe them in tears, for lo, my feet have been as lead. Lo, they have been weighted down with the cares of this life. For I have been as one in a dream who seeketh to run and is held in paralysis.

Set me free, Omnipotent Lord, and make me Thy glad and willing bond slave. Loose my feet and make them swift to do thy bidding. Loose my tongue to shout Thy praise. Loose my heart to love the lost with the great deep compassion of Jesus Christ. Yea, free mine affections, and nail them to Thy cross! Amen.

# Rivers of Living Water

*I will lift up mine eyes unto the hills, from whence cometh my help. My help cometh from the LORD, which made heaven and earth.*

PSALM 121:1–2

Behold, thou art in the hollow of Mine hand. Yea, in the moment that thou liftest thy voice to cry unto Me, and when thou raiseth thy voice to praise and magnify My Name, THEN shall My glory gather thee up. Yea, I will wrap thee in the garments of joy, and My presence shall be thy great reward.

Lift thine eyes to Mine. Thou shalt know of a surety that I love thee. Lift thy voice to Me in praise: so shall a fountain be opened within thee and thou shalt drink of its refreshing waters.

Pour out thy heart unto Me. From the deepest recesses of thy being, let thy love flow forth unto Me; let thy lips utter My Name.

# Rivers of Living Water
## PART 2

*Jesus stood and cried, saying,*
*If any man thirst, let him come unto*
*me, and drink. He that believeth on*
*me, as the scripture hath said, out of*
*his belly shall flow rivers of living water.*

JOHN 7:37-38

Behold, thou art in Mine embrace. REST THERE. For My Spirit and My ways are not to be mastered by intellect, but My love is to be received by those who long after Me and who reciprocate in kind. For so as faith receiveth the promises, and those who seek after eternal life are recipients of the faith of Jesus Christ (for faith is the *gift* of God) even so, they who long for a closer relationship with Me, to them shall I give a special portion of My love that they may have the power to love Me in return as I have loved them.

# Give Me a Drink

*And this voice which came from heaven we heard, when we were with him in the holy mount.*

2 PETER 1:18

Behold, the time is short. Be not entangled in the things of the world, for they are transitory. Be not over-concerned as to thy personal needs, for your Heavenly Father knoweth what ye have need of, and He will supply. But let thine uppermost concern be to carry out My will and purpose for thy life, to be sensitive to My guidance, and to keep thine ear open toward Heaven.

*Miss anything else, but don't miss My voice.* Other voices may introduce disharmony, but My voice will always bring peace to thy heart and clarity to thy thinking. For ye shall hear My voice behind thee saying: This is the way, walk ye in it, when thou turnest to the left hand or to the right.

# Give Me a Drink
## PART 2

*Give, and it shall be given unto you;*
*good measure, pressed down, and*
*shaken together, and running over,*
*shall men give into your bosom.*

LUKE 6:38

Yea, I will keep thee in the center of My will and My being, lest on the one hand ye move into coldness and doubt, or on the other hand ye be carried away by fleshly zeal. But there is no neutrality in the center. This is not an arbitrary position. For I will fill thee with the abundance of My own life.

Thy heart will burn with the Fire of My Love. Thou shalt rejoice in all kinds of circumstances, because I will share with thee My joy; and My joy is completely disassociated with the world and with the people of the world. But I joy in those who joy in Me. My love I pour out to those who pour out their lives to Me.

# I Will Bring the Victory

*For whatsoever is born of God overcometh
the world: and this is the victory that
overcometh the world, even our faith.*

1 JOHN 5:4

*I have protected* thee and kept thee in sickness and in health. Yea, I am with thee to help thee now. Fear not. My purposes will be fulfilled in spite of thy weaknesses, if in thy need ye rely on My strength.

My will shall be done regardless of the flaws in thy life, if ye count upon the power of My righteousness. I do not work only in cases where there are no obstacles; but I glory in over-ruling the prevailing circumstances, and I take pleasure in bringing victories in those places where no victory is anywhere in sight. . . .

Ask for the victory. I will come and bring it. *Don't look for the victory—look for Me*, and ye shall see the victory that I shall bring with Me.

# Cleanse the Sanctuary

*Sing and rejoice, O daughter of Zion:*
*for, lo, I come, and I will dwell in*
*the midst of thee, saith the LORD.*

ZECHARIAH 2:10

WITH A WHOLE Heart have I commanded that ye love Me and that ye serve Me with Undivided Loyalty. Ye cannot serve two masters. Purge out, therefore, the old leaven, and make clean the vessels. Cleanse the Sanctuary, and bring Me thy sacrifices with pure hearts and clean hands. . . .

For I long after thee with a love that embraces Eternity. Though thou goest astray, I will surely draw thee back. Though thy love grow cold and thine heart indifferent, if thou shalt listen, thou shalt surely hear My voice. When thou turnest to Me, I shall bridge the gap. For though ye have strayed, I have not left thee. Wherever ye turn to Me in love and confession, lo, I am there in the midst of thee.

# Courage

*And David said to Solomon his son,*
*Be strong and of good courage, and do it:*
*fear not, nor be dismayed: for the Lord*
*God, even my God, will be with thee.*

1 CHRONICLES 28:20

My people shall not go mourning, for I the Lord shall be their rejoicing and their song. They shall not be a complaining people, for I shall take away the murmuring from your streets. . . .

I shall give to My people brave and courageous spirits, and I will make them strong of heart. I will give them the spirit of the martyrs, for they shall be My witnesses of resurrection power. They shall be stalwart. They shall be steadfast. And I shall remove from the ranks those who are timid and those who desire comfort and security. My way is a way of sacrifice, and the rewards are not in worldly honors.

# Courage
## PART 2

*But let us, who are of the day, be sober,*
*putting on the breastplate of faith and love;*
*and for an helmet, the hope of salvation.*

1 THESSALONIANS 5:8

As it is written: "Even Christ pleased not himself" (Romans 15:3). How dare ye risk allowing the flesh to manifest its desires? They can be only evil continually. No good thing can come out of a deceitful heart. "The arm of flesh will fail you—ye dare not trust your own."

Only that which is generated within thee by the Spirit of God can bring forth righteousness; and be not conformed unto this world, but be becoming transformed by the renewing of your minds that ye may personally discover what is the good and acceptable and perfect will of God.

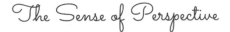

# The Sense of Perspective

*Love your enemies, bless them that curse
you, do good to them that hate you,
and pray for them which despitefully
use you, and persecute you.*

MATTHEW 5:44

Who know better than My children the crimes
of the world? Have not many of them been
perpetrated against you yourselves, even whilst
ye sought to serve and worship Me? For mankind resisteth My hand upon them. But how can
they punish *Me*? They can most naturally express their hostility toward the Almighty and
show their resentment against My laws by ill-
treating My children. Shall ye not be called to
witness against them?

. . .Today is the day of My grace, and it
operateth through thee also, bringing loving
forgiveness to all, even the spirit manifest by
Jesus as He hung upon the cross. But the day of
judgment shall be a day of strict reckoning.

# The Sense of Perspective
## PART 2

*Eye hath not seen, nor ear heard,
neither have entered into the heart
of man, the things which God hath
prepared for them that love him.*

1 CORINTHIANS 2:9

Do you fear calamity? Ye are only human if ye do. But have ye considered My servant the apostle Paul? In shipwrecks, in adversities, in distresses, in physical privations, in persecutions and threat of death by wild beasts; in all of these, he rejoiced in his God. He was more than victorious. He was given a supernatural joy in the midst of all his distresses. Ye may have it too. . . .

If ye can catch the vision of what the days ahead hold in store for thee in My great Kingdom, you will gain a whole new perspective, so that as ye view the present, transient scene, it will come into clear focus as to its true dimension in proportion to the whole panoramic picture.

# The Sense of Perspective
## PART 3

*That the God of our Lord Jesus Christ,
the Father of glory, may give unto you
the spirit of wisdom and revelation
in the knowledge of him.*

EPHESIANS 1:17

*I can give* you the sense of perspective, because I see the whole scroll of the ages as it were already unrolled before Me—so that the future is as clearly in view as the past. Look over My shoulder! Look at your own life from My vantage point. My Spirit will bring thee revelation and understanding, light and wisdom.

The man of mature years has gained wisdom by experience. Ye may gain wisdom (if ye desire it) by, as it were, drawing on My experience. I am infinite and eternal, and though ye may be unable to grasp it, I have experienced both what is known to you as the past and what is referred to by you as the future.

# Remove the Rocks

*Have mercy upon me, O God, according
to thy lovingkindness: according unto
the multitude of thy tender mercies
blot out my transgressions.*

PSALM 51:1

Behold, after the weeds are cleared; after the fallow ground is broken up; yea, after the rocks have been removed: *Then will I send the showers*, and then will I minister to thy hearts in kindness and in blessing. For though My heart hath been grieved, yet I love thee; and though I have hid My face from thee for a time, lo, in great tenderness would I gather thee again unto Myself.

I will withhold My chastening rod when ye turn unto Me in repentance. If ye confess thy sins and recognize thy transgressions, I will be faithful to thee and forgive thee. I will cleanse and restore thee. Thou wilt find peace. Thou shalt say the tears of godly sorrow have been sweet.

# Put Away the Idols

*And I will give them an heart to know me,*
*that I am the Lord: and they shall be my*
*people, and I will be their God: for they shall*
*return unto me with their whole heart.*

JEREMIAH 24:7

I have put My Spirit upon thee that thou shouldest cry and not keep silence. I have spoken unto thee that thou mightest. . .understand what is in My heart.

For I love My people, yea, My chosen and elect; and Mine heart grieveth over them, because they are turned aside. They have known My love; yea, they have tasted of My goodness, and entered into My grace, and My salvation have I given unto them; but their love hath waxed cold, and their desires have been turned to others, and their ways are the paths of self-seeking and folly.

For I am a jealous God, saith Jehovah, and I will not share My glory with another.

# Put Away the Idols
## PART 2

*Come, and let us return unto the LORD:*
*for he hath torn, and he will heal us;*
*he hath smitten, and he will bind us up.*

HOSEA 6:1

BUT MY PEOPLE Have Not Cried: they have not called. Lo, they have been satisfied with the husks of this present world, and in an hour of indifference, they have allowed the pleasures of this life to fill that place which belongeth only unto Me. Yea, it hath displaced My Spirit, but it satisfieth not.

O that they might return unto Me, saith the Lord, for as the father waited the return of the prodigal, so long I for My people. . . .

Return unto Me, saith the Lord, and I will return unto you. PUT AWAY THE IDOLS, and give Me thy heart. Lay thine heart open before Me, and I will purge away the dross. I will cleanse it and fill it with My glory.

# Saturate Thy Soul in the Oil of the Spirit

*For he satisfieth the longing soul, and filleth
the hungry soul with goodness.*

PSALM 107:9

Do not imagine for a moment that I can do any mighty works in the atmosphere of hostility and evil and rebellion. Come unto Me with a cleansed heart and a right spirit: in sincerity, in honesty. If ye desire Me to work in thy midst, do not be devious in thy ways nor indirect in thy dealings with others (2 Corinthians 4:2). It is the pure in heart who see God. It is those who seek after a holy walk and who set their heart toward holy living who inherit the promises and who come into My holy hill.

…Where there is the activity of the Almighty, there are forces of Life continually working to produce within thee a measure of the life and health and strength which are in Him.

# Saturate Thy Soul in the Oil of the Spirit
## PART 2

*The Lord is my strength and song,*
*and he is become my salvation.*

EXODUS 15:2

Why will ye tolerate any idea of discouragement? Nothing can ever be accomplished for good in this frame of mind. Sin bringeth forth death; and any negative current flowing within thy body shall produce a steady regression.

I will prepare within thee a different attitude of mind. Thoughts that have been in confusion, I will reorganize. I will not bring to bear upon thee pressures that will cause thee to be weak. I will be to thee the strength which ye need. I will be to thee the inner fortification which will bear thee up even in the time of strain and crisis.

SATURATE THY SOUL IN THE OIL OF THE HOLY SPIRIT, *and keep thy channel of communication ever open to thy Heavenly Father.* His desire is toward thee, and He will be thy strong habitation.

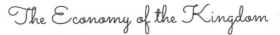

# The Economy of the Kingdom

*Bring ye all the tithes into the storehouse,*
*that there may be meat in mine house, and*
*prove me now herewith, saith the LORD of*
*hosts, if I will not open you the windows of*
*heaven, and pour you out a blessing, that*
*there shall not be room enough to receive it.*

MALACHI 3:10

Ye shall never give unto Me and become the poorer for it. Ye shall be given in exchange for thy small gifts My boundless riches, and through the contribution that cometh from a willing heart I shall be freed to bestow out of the abundance of heaven treasures ye could never with money purchase from the world.

But see that thy giving is with joyfulness—for God delighteth in a cheerful giver. . . . As ye have received freely even so it is required of thee that thou give without grudging, nor be mindful of any sacrifice.

# The Economy of the Kingdom
## PART 2

*Give, and it shall be given unto you;*
*good measure, pressed down, and*
*shaken together, and running over,*
*shall men give into your bosom.*

LUKE 6:38

Be My agents of righteousness and good will, and I shall prove Myself to thee as thy loving Heavenly Father, supplying thy needs out of the riches of My own treasury—and this, too, shall be to thee an exciting adventure in thy walk in the Spirit.

For ye shall see in what miraculous ways I will care for thy needs, and even in the process of doing this will further yet more the Kingdom; for others in giving to you shall receive spiritual blessings.

Yes, My child, My economy is wonderful! My Kingdom truly is not the kingdom of the world. . . .

Give, My children. Thy poverty shall be turned to wealth, and thou shalt be freed from thine anxieties concerning financial matters.

# Household Salvation

*Yea, I have loved thee with an*
*everlasting love: therefore with*
*lovingkindness have I drawn thee.*

JEREMIAH 31:3

With strong cords have I bound thee to Me. In the day of adversity I have been thy refuge, and in the hour of need I have holden thee up, and thou hast found thy strength in Me. Thou hast seen My goodness on the right hand and on the left. Thou hast beheld My power, and My glory has not been hid from thee. . . .

So renew thine energies, and know that I am working with thee. For surely a light shall shine out of the darkness, and the faith thou hast exercised through the years shall be rewarded an hundred-fold. So thy faith shall be turned to sight; for thou shalt see with thine eyes and hear with thine ears and rejoice in thine heart over that thing which shall come to pass.

# Household Salvation

## PART 2

*Hear me, O LORD; for thy lovingkindness
is good: turn unto me according to the
multitude of thy tender mercies.*

PSALM 69:16

*I have blessed* thee out of the bounties of heaven and have not withheld from thee ought of what thy heart hath desired. Yea, and I would yet do more. For have I not promised that thou shouldest be saved AND thy household? . . .

I will do a wonderful work, and thou shalt praise and glorify My name *together*! For He that keepeth thee neither slumbers nor sleeps. The Lord thy God is thy strength, and in Him is no weariness. He tireth not at thy coming, and thy cry is welcome to His ears however frequent.

Cast thyself upon His mercies; for His loving-kindness never faileth, and His grace and compassion are inexhaustible. His faithfulness is extended to all generations (Psalm 89:1).

# I Shall Gather My People

*He cometh with clouds; and every*
*eye shall see him, and they also which*
*pierced him: and all kindreds of the*
*earth shall wail because of him.*

REVELATION 1:7

Lift thine eyes to the clouds; for lo, the heavens are filled with glory. He cometh with ten thousand of His saints. Lift thine hearts, for thou shalt not be afraid because of those things which are coming to pass upon the earth. FOR I SHALL GATHER MY PEOPLE UNTO MYSELF; and in the hour of destruction, I will stretch forth Mine hand to deliver them. In the hour of wrath, I will snatch away My own—My Beloved—and the flames shall not touch them.

. . .For though nation rise against nation, and though war break forth into a universal holocaust; yea, though mankind in its folly dasheth itself to bits against the wall of the inevitable, yet have I not changed, saith the Lord God.

## Check Thy Course

*O LORD: let thy lovingkindness and*
*thy truth continually preserve me.*

PSALM 40:11

*Go not into* the path of folly, for My heart goeth with thee wheresoever thou goest; and I grieve over thee when thou art turned aside. Ye may not be going in the opposite direction. Ye may even be on a road that lies quite parallel with the one upon which I would have thee travel. But to be *almost* in the perfect will of God is to miss it completely.

CHECK THY COURSE. Chart it by My Word, and hold to it with rigid determination and be not led aside by the other little ships. . . .

Be sure you are in the boat with Him if ye hope to make it safe to shore in spite of the storms. For there shall be storms; but ye shall be safe if ye abide close with Me.

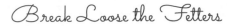

## Break Loose the Fetters

*When thou goest, thy steps shall
not be straitened; and when thou
runnest, thou shalt not stumble.*

PROVERBS 4:12

Through the Red Seas, through the Wildernesses, through the Jordans, through the Promised Lands of spiritual conquest—I am with My people. *Let no fear dismay.* Let no aspect of the Past be a hindrance or stumbling block. For I bring you out of traditions of the past into Living Reality. I bring you out of traditions of the past into fresh revelations of Myself in this Present Hour.

The Past I use for thine instruction, but not as a blueprint of the present nor guidance for the future. . . .

What manner of men ought ye to be with such a prospect in view!

BREAK LOOSE THE FETTER. Cast off the fears. Walk forth in Me in the conquering strength of My Holy Spirit.

## A Garden of Fountains

*Behold, the LORD's hand is not shortened,*
*that it cannot save; neither his ear*
*heavy, that it cannot hear.*

ISAIAH 59:1

Behold, My hand is upon thee to bless thee and to accomplish all My good purpose. For *this hour* I have prepared thy heart; and in My kindness I will not let thee fail.

Only relinquish *all things* into My hands; for I can work freely *only as ye release Me by complete committal*—both of thyself and others. Even as was written of old: "*Commit* thy way unto the LORD; trust also in him; and he shall bring it to pass" (Psalm 37:5). I will be thy sustaining strength; and My peace shall garrison thy mind. Only TRUST ME—that all I do is done in love.

# A Garden of Fountains
## PART 2

*And the LORD shall guide thee continually,
and satisfy thy soul in drought, and make
fat thy bones: and thou shalt be like a
watered garden, and like a spring of
water, whose waters fail not.*

ISAIAH 58:11

For adversities must of necessity come. They are part of the pattern of life's pilgrimage for every individual; and who can escape them? But I say unto thee, that for those who walk in Me, and for those who are encircled by the intercessory prayers of My children, I shall make of the suffering, yea, I shall make of the trials a steppingstone to future blessing (2 Corinthians 4:17–18, Living Letters).

My arms are around thee, and never have I loved thee more! I will make thee like A GARDEN OF FOUNTAINS whose streams are fed by the mountain springs.

# Launch Out!

*Cast thy burden upon the LORD,*
*and he shall sustain thee: he shall*
*never suffer the righteous to be moved.*

PSALM 55:22

Thus saith the Lord unto His people:

Lo, ye have touched only the fringes.

Yea, thou hast lingered upon the shore lines.

Launch out, yea, launch out upon the vast bosom of My love and mercy, yea,

My mighty power and limitless resources.

For lo, if thou wouldst enter into all that I have for thee, thou must walk by faith upon the waters.

Thou must relinquish forever thy doubts;

and thy thoughts of self-preservation thou must forever cast aside.

For I will carry thee, and I will sustain thee by My power in the ways that I have chosen and prepared for thee.

Thou shalt not take even the first step in thine own strength.

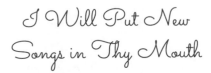

# I Will Put New Songs in Thy Mouth

*And he hath put a new song in my mouth,*
*even praise unto our God: many shall see it,*
*and fear, and shall trust in the Lord.*

PSALM 40:3

O my soul, wait thou upon God, and He will do thee good.

Yea, He will be to thee refreshing to thy soul. . . .

. . .For I shall fill thy soul with fatness, and I will be with thee to do thee good. I will make thy hands to war, and I will make thy lips to praise Me with songs.

I will put new songs in thy mouth, and thou shalt rejoice in the Lord thy God for He is a Mighty God.

He delivereth, and no man can bind:

He lifteth up and none can pull down.

Yea, He doeth valiantly, and who can prevent Him?

# Rain

*For the earth which drinketh in the rain
that cometh oft upon it, and bringeth forth
herbs meet for them by whom it is dressed,
receiveth blessing from God.*

HEBREWS 6:7

O My child, I love thee, I love thee.

Get thee to the hills and look, for lo, there cometh rain.

The drought is over and past, and the sound of rain approacheth!

Yea, I will send showers of blessing upon the hearts of my waiting people; for before they call, I have prepared to answer, and while they are seeking Me, I shall come down upon them.

O Lord, tarry not. We wait for Thee.

We long for Thee. Yea, our souls pant for Thee as the thirsting deer panteth for the waterbrooks.

## Rain

### PART 2

*For as the rain cometh down, and the snow
from heaven, and returneth not thither, but
watereth the earth, and maketh it bring forth
and bud, that it may give seed to the sower,
and bread to the eater.*

ISAIAH 55:10

Lift thine eyes to the heavens, for lo, they are filled with clouds; yea, they are heavy with water.

Get thee back to the camp.

Set out the buckets and make preparation: for already the wind rises, the leaves rustle in the trees; the birds hasten to their nests, and lo, I come. I come to revive and to refresh. I come to quicken and to cleanse. I come as floods upon parched ground. So shall new life spring forth, and the desert shall be filled with flowers.

For since time was, have I never forsaken My people. I have undertaken for them; I have protected them.

I have delivered them in every time of need.

# Rain

## PART 3

*For thou art an holy people unto the LORD thy God: the LORD thy God hath chosen thee to be a special people unto himself, above all people that are upon the face of the earth.*

DEUTERONOMY 7:6

Shall I not shed My love upon thee for no other reason than simply that I have CHOSEN so to do?

Otherwise were it not love in its purest sense.

For only as thou knowest with certainty that I love thee *though thou bring no gift*, can ye return to Me love that will remain constant both when I bless, and when I withhold.

. . .Gather me in Thine embrace, for Thine arms are stronger than the bands of Orion.

All eternity is held in one moment in Thy presence, and all of time is vanity apart from Thy fellowship.

# A Song at Midnight

*Rejoice not against me, O mine enemy:*
*when I fall, I shall arise; when I sit in*
*darkness, the Lord shall be a light unto me.*

### MICAH 7:8

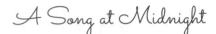

For My heart is open to thy cry; yea, when thou criest unto Me in the night seasons, I am alert to thy call, and when thou searchest after Me, the darkness shall not hide My face. . . .

Even so shall it be. And in the night of spiritual battle, there shall I give unto thee fresh revelations of Myself, and thou shalt see Me more clearly than thou couldst in the sunlight of ease and pleasure.

Man by nature chooseth the day and shunneth the night; but I say unto thee

that I shall make thy midnight a time of great rejoicing, and I will fill the dark hour with songs of praise.

# Keep Thy Face toward the Sunrise

*Enter thou into the joy of thy lord.*

MATTHEW 25:23

*I will turn* the bitter tear to sweet perfume.

By My Spirit, I will mend the broken heart.

I will pour warm, fragrant oil into the deep wound.

For Mine heart is fused with thy heart, and in thy grief, I am one with thee.

Yea, I will fill the vacant place.

Mine arms shall hold thee, and thou shalt not fall.

My grace shall sustain thee, and thou shalt not faint. My joy shall fortify thy spirit even as a broken body is rejuvenated by a blood transfusion.

My smile shall dispel the shadows, and My voice shall speak courage.

Yea, I will surely keep thee, and thou shalt not know fear.

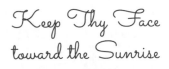

# Keep Thy Face toward the Sunrise

## PART 2

*Nevertheless for thy great mercies'
sake thou didst not utterly consume
them, nor forsake them; for thou art
a gracious and merciful God.*

NEHEMIAH 9:31

Thou shalt rest thy foot upon the threshold of heaven. . . .

I will not leave thee for a moment. I will keep thee from despair: I will deliver thee from confusion. When thou art perplexed, I will guide thee in wisdom and in judgment.

By thy light shall others be led out of the valley. By thy courage shall the weak be lifted up.

By thy steadfastness shall he that wavereth be stabilized.

Lo, the hour is upon thee. Look not back.

Keep thy face toward the sunrise, for He shall rise fresh daily in thy soul with healing in His wings.

# Your Body, a Living Sacrifice

*My son, keep my words, and lay up my commandments with thee.*

PROVERBS 7:1

Behold, I say unto thee: Yield Me your body as a living sacrifice, and be not conformed to the things of the world, but be ye transformed by the renewal of your mind.

Set your affections on things of the Spirit, and be not in bondage to the desires of the flesh.

For I have purchased you at great price.

Yea, thou art My very special possession and My treasure.

I would have thee to set thine affections and desires upon Me even as I have set Mine heart upon thee....

For I must have a vessel through which to operate.

I would have you to be a vessel not only yielded to Me, but purified, dedicated, sanctified for My use; available to Me at all times, and ready to be used at whatever time I have need of thee.

# Your Body, a Living Sacrifice
## PART 2

*Keep yourselves in the love of God,*
*looking for the mercy of our Lord*
*Jesus Christ unto eternal life.*

JUDE 21

Thou wilt not have time to make thyself ready when I need thee.

Thou must be already prepared.

Thou must keep thyself in a state of readiness.

Thou canst not live to the flesh and at the same time be available to the Spirit.

Ye must walk in the Spirit, and in so doing keep thyself from becoming entangled in the things of the flesh.

Ye must live in obedience to the Spirit,

and thus be kept from being in bondage to the desires of the flesh. . . .

By setting your soul *through deliberate choice of your will* to pursue the worship of God by praying in the Spirit, thou shalt find thy faith strengthened and thy life bathed in the love of God.

# Your Body, a Living Sacrifice
## PART 3

*And ye became followers of us, and of the Lord, having received the word in much affliction, with joy of the Holy Ghost.*

1 THESSALONIANS 1:6

With thy faith laying hold upon God's promises and power, and thine actions motivated by the love of God, thou wilt find thyself in the path of the *activity of God*:

His blessing shall be upon thee, and He will accomplish His works through thee.

Thou needest make no plans nor resort to any clever strategy.

Keep yourself in the love of God. . . .

For as thine own spirit is aware when His Spirit is grieved within thee, so shalt thou also be aware when His Spirit *rejoices* within thee. This is His joy. This is the joy He promised.

This is the greatest joy that can come to the human heart, for it is the joy of God, and the joy of God transcends the joy of man.

# Conviction and Forgiveness

*Thou hast made known to me the
ways of life; thou shalt make me
full of joy with thy countenance.*

ACTS 2:28

My patience is running to an end, saith the Lord. For I have purposed and man hath despised. I have planned, and man hath set at naught. I have willed and ye have resisted Me. Be not smug in your own ways; for your ways are not My ways, saith the Lord.

Ye are indulgent when I have called you to rigid discipline. Ye speak soft words when I would require of thee to speak the truth. Ye interfere with the convicting work of My Holy Spirit when ye smooth over confession. I am not a severe God, unmindful of the frailties of human nature, but I am a God of divine love and holiness, and I desire your fellowship, and I long for you to know the joy of Mine.

# Conviction and Forgiveness
## PART 2

*Jesus saith unto him, I am the way,
the truth, and the life: no man cometh
unto the Father, but by me.*

JOHN 14:6

Man cannot forgive sin. Why do ye then excuse either thyself or thy brother? Before Me ye stand or fall. Confess your faults one to another, and pray for one another that ye may be perfected. Rebuke, warn, and exhort each other with all long-suffering and patience. Love and forgive each other, but do not lighten conviction.

My love and My holiness are beyond your comprehension. I do not love you because you are sinless (how then could I love any?) but I am able to receive you into My fellowship and bring you close to My heart on the merits of the shed blood of the Lord Jesus Christ. Here only rests your hope of cleansing and acceptance. Here is the only door of access between sinful man and a holy God.

# Look Not Back

*I press toward the mark for the prize of the
high calling of God in Christ Jesus.*

PHILIPPIANS 3:14

Thine every hair is numbered, and the most incidental occurrences of the most ordinary day

I delight to choose and use to reveal to thee
My earnestness in helping thee.

Clasp Me to thine heart, for I love thee with an everlasting love, and with strong cords have I bound thee.

Look not back, but look ahead, for I have glory prepared for thee.

Yea, when thou lookest on My face thou wilt surely say that these present sufferings are in no way comparable to the glory which I have in store for thee.

# Fling Aside Thy Fears

*Whosoever shall not receive the*
*kingdom of God as a little child*
*shall in no wise enter therein.*

LUKE 18:17

Lo, I have sought thee, following thee upon the hills and pursuing thee through the barren wastes.

Yea, I have called after thee, but thou hast not heard. . . .

. . .For My ways are hid to those who seek Me in impatience, and the eyes which seek Me in human wisdom shall never find Me.

. . .For when thou art utterly finished and exhausted in thy struggling; when thou hast come to an end in all thy striving; when thou art ready to desert thine intellectual pursuit, and when thou shalt cast thyself upon Me as a babe upon its mother's breast; *then* shalt thou know surely that I have been constantly at thy very side; that I have never deserted thee.

# Fling Aside Thy Fears

## PART 2

*I sought the LORD, and he heard me,*
*and delivered me from all my fears.*

PSALM 34:4

Yea, that My love for thee is of such nature and intensity that it would be impossible that thou couldst ever escape My thoughts, or that My longing after thee could ever waver.

Cast aside thy questionings.

Fling aside thy fears.

For surely Mine arms are already outstretched to receive thee.

Only believe.

For in the moment that thou relinquish *all*—in that same moment shalt thou know release.

For thou shalt be set free of thyself and thou shalt be captive of My love.

Mine arms shall gather thee, and I shall never let thee go!

# Be Not Afraid

*Fear not, O land; be glad and rejoice:*
*for the Lord will do great things.*

JOEL 2:21

Yea, quietly settle down in My care, as a bird settles in a nest.

For I am watching over thee, and in love will I care for thee.

There is no danger with which I am unable to cope.

There is no enemy too formidable for Me to handle.

I am able to carry out all My purposes, and to keep thee at the same time.

Be not afraid; neither allow terror to strike at thy heart.

My power is at thy disposal.

My presence standeth round about thee, and nothing can harm thee so long as ye are in My care, and that is forever. . . .

# Seize Each Opportunity

*Boast not thyself of to morrow; for thou knowest not what a day may bring forth.*

PROVERBS 27:1

Behold, as the lilies of the field, and as the grass, so thy life is but for a season.

Yea, though thou flourish in health, yet is thy time short.

Thou hast no sure promise of tomorrow.

Therefore live each day as though it were thy last.

*Seize each opportunity* knowing it may be the last.

For it is verily true that no situation presents itself twice the same. The opportunities of today are not those of tomorrow.

Live not as though they might be repeated.

Fail not to enter every open door. Be not held back by a feeling of unreadiness. I Myself am thy preparation.

# Seize Each Opportunity
## PART 2

*And now, Lord, what wait I for?*
*my hope is in thee.*

PSALM 39:7

For I will give to thee the needed grace and wisdom for each moment as it cometh, and thou shalt rejoice in the victory.

For I will overcome timidity, and I Myself will displace inadequacy.

This is *My* work. I will do it Myself through thee if thou but allow thyself to be a channel for the flow of My Spirit.

For I Myself am the life. I Myself am thy wisdom and thy strength, even as I am thy joy and thy peace.

I am thy victory. My word is power because My word is spirit and truth.

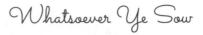

# Whatsoever Ye Sow

*He which soweth sparingly shall reap also*
*sparingly; and he which soweth bountifully*
*shall reap also bountifully.*

2 CORINTHIANS 9:6

How can I give you healing for your body whilst there is anxiety in thy mind? So long as there is disease in thy thoughts, there shall be disease in thy body. Ye have need of many things, but one thing in particular ye must develop for thine own preservation, and that is an absolute confidence in My loving care.

"Come unto me," it is written, "all ye that labour and are heavy laden, and I will give you rest" (Matthew 11:28). Only when your mind is at rest can your body build health. Worry is an actively destructive force. Anxiety produces tension, and tension is the road to pain. Fear is devastating to the physical well-being of the body. Anger throws poison into the system that no antibiotic ever can counteract.

# Whatsoever Ye Sow
## PART 2

*For as he thinketh in his heart, so is he.*
PROVERBS 23:7

You cannot risk giving your thoughts free rein. They will never choose the right path until you bridle them and control them by your own disciplined will. You are master of your own house. You do not have to invite into your mind the foul birds of evil thoughts and allow them to nest there and bring forth their young.

Whatsoever ye do in your secret thought-life, that shall ye reap. Sow love and kindness, and ye shall be rewarded openly. Sow charity and forgiveness, and ye shall reap in kind. Sow generosity and gratitude, and ye shall never feel poor. Sow hope, and ye shall reap fulfillment. Sow praise, and ye shall reap joy and well-being and a strong faith. Sow bountifully, and ye shall reap bountifully. Sow! Ye shall see your seed and be satisfied.

# The Last Great Outpouring

*I will pour water upon him that is thirsty,
and floods upon the dry ground: I will
pour my spirit upon thy seed, and my
blessing upon thine offspring.*

ISAIAH 44:3

*I will pour* out My Spirit, and by prophecies, by signs and wonders, by many different types of miracles, and by healings. . . . I am the Alpha and the Omega. Stand firm in Me. Never waver.

Be faithful regardless of apparent failures and discouragements; for My word shall surely be fulfilled, and thine eyes shall see Revival in proportion like as has never been witnessed before in the history of the human race.

Keep your eye on the end of the course. Victory is secured already. Do not let the hurdles cause thee consternation. Stay in the running. I am at thy side. According to each day shall thy strength be; and the race is not to the swift, but the obedient shall receive the prize.

# Sing, My Children

*God is not a man, that he should lie; neither the son of man, that he should repent: hath he said, and shall he not do it? or hath he spoken, and shall he not make it good?*

NUMBERS 23:19

Remember that I am in the midst when ye praise Me. Never let any kind of anxiety crowd out thy praises. Do not be concerned for My reputation. I have withstood many a storm, and I will survive this one. Man's strivings are as the waters around Gibraltar. They have beat upon the rock, but they have not changed it. I am not disturbed, and I forbid thee to be anxious.

For anxiety gendereth to tension, and tension erodes joy; and when joy is gone, victory is lost, faith is weakened, and spontaneity is destroyed. . . .

Sing, My children, and let the shout of praise be heard; for the Lord is mighty, and His Name is glorious.

## Quiet Pool

*He maketh me to lie down in green pastures:*
*he leadeth me beside the still waters.*

PSALM 23:2

Lo, I say unto thee, Wait upon ME.

Let thy life be as a deep, quiet pool.

Yea, let thine heart rest in Mine hand as a bird in a nest.

Let thine eyes be still. Let thine hands be free.

For then shall I fill all thy vision, and then shall I take thine hands into Mine and My power shall flow forth unto thee.

Only make unto thyself a place apart; yea, a place removed from the press and turmoil, and there will I meet thee. Yea I wait thy coming.

For I long to pour out my blessings upon thee, and I long to give thee of my fulness.

Only be thou still before Me.

# Quiet Pool

## PART 2

*The LORD will perfect that which concerneth
me: thy mercy, O LORD, endureth for ever:
forsake not the works of thine own hands.*

PSALM 138:8

Let not the toils and cares of the day rob thee
of this sweet fellowship with Me.

For I know what things ye have need of,
and I am concerned about thine every duty and
responsibility.

But thou wilt find thy cares have vanished
and thy load lightened as by an unseen hand.

For I will that ye bring Me thy love, and even
as thou art bringing to Me thy love,

I shall in turn bring to thee My power, so that
I work for thee in a two-fold measure.

For I give unto thee the power to discharge
thy duties with greater efficiency, and I also am
actively engaged in working for thee in ways thou
canst not see, to make thy path clear, and to bring
about things which thou thyself couldest never
accomplish, and which would otherwise absorb
thine energies and wear out thy patience.

## Call of the Turtledove

*Deep calleth unto deep at the noise*
*of thy waterspouts: all thy waves*
*and thy billows are gone over me.*

PSALM 42:7

O My children, there is the sound of the turtledove going throughout the land. It is the voice of the Bridegroom calling forth His Bride. It is the wooing of the Spirit bringing forth a people for His Name. Yea, it is the Lord of Glory, Jesus Christ Himself, drawing together them that are His. It is the call of love, and they who truly love Him shall respond. . . .

I tell you, there shall be a revelation of My nearness given to My dear ones before My second coming.

Anticipate Me. Watch for Me. Thy heart shall listen, and thy heart shall hear. I am not far off. I am looking through the lattice (Song of Solomon 2:9). Ye shall see Me—ye shall know—ye shall rejoice.

## Love Never Faileth

*Charity never faileth: but whether there be prophecies, they shall fail; whether there be tongues, they shall cease; whether there be knowledge, it shall vanish away.*

1 CORINTHIANS 13:8

Behold, I am the Lord, *Thy* God; is *anything* too hard for Me? I am the LIGHT of the world, and the greatest darkness shall never be able to quench that light. I shall be to thee a cloud to preserve by day and a pillar of fire to protect by night. Both in the sunshine and in the darkness, I shall be near thee. Thou shalt delight in Me in thy joys; and in the place of difficulty My love for thee shall be as inescapably real as a blazing pillar of fire. Yea, all I was to Israel, and more, I shall be to thee. For have I not promised to give thee the desires of thine heart, and the heathen for thine inheritance?

## Love Never Faileth

### PART 2

*And now abideth faith, hope, charity, these three; but the greatest of these is charity.*

1 CORINTHIANS 13:13

Let no fear hinder. For he that wavereth receiveth not. But keep thine heart single and every alien thought thou shalt rebuke in My Name, for it is of the enemy. For he knoweth full well that he has no defense against pure faith. Only if he can succeed to plant some seed of doubt can he hold back the blessing of heaven among the people of God and nullify the witness to the lost. So hold fast thy profession of faith, for there is a great recompense of reward. (Or we may say, the inheritance of faith is a most rewarding recompense.)

So praise Me continually, for *Praise* worketh *Faith,* and *God inhabiteth the Praise of His People.* . . . Be sure of this: *LOVE NEVER FAILETH.* Loving Me never fails to bring Me to thy side.

# Hold Fast

*Which hope we have as an anchor of the soul,
both sure and stedfast..*

HEBREWS 6:19

Hold fast that which thou hast, and let no man take thy crown.

Let no man hinder thee in pursuit of the reward. Let nothing stand in the way of thy complete victory. Let no weariness or discouraging thought cause thee to unloose the rope of faith, but bind it the tighter and anchor fast to My Word.

For My Word can never fail, yea, and all My good promises I will surely fulfill.

Have not I said, "He that seeketh shall find"? And have not I promised to be the rewarder of them that diligently seek Me?

Not of the dilatory seeker, but of the diligent seeker. Not of him whose seeking is in reality only wishing, but of him who has grown so intent in his quest that he has become wholly absorbed to the extent that he is unmindful in his toiling of the sweat upon his brow.

# Thou Hast Run into My Arms

*Charity shall cover the multitude of sins.*

1 PETER 4:8

O My child, thou hast thought in thine heart that thou wouldst run from Me. But lo, I am everywhere before thee, and thou hast only run into My arms. For I care for thee—yea, I think upon thee constantly, and I seek to do thee good.

Thou fearest My rod of correction, but as it is written, it is the love of God that causes men to repent. Take My love, and in the taking, thy heart shall be so warmed and made tender, and at the same time encouraged and made strong, that ye will not need the rod, nor anticipate My displeasure.

For if it be so that human love covereth a multitude of sins how much more is it true of the divine love of God the Father!

# Lie Not Dormant

*This man was instructed in the way of the
Lord; and being fervent in the spirit, he spake
and taught diligently the things of the Lord,
knowing only the baptism of John.*

ACTS 18:25

My child, I have need of thee. Without thy
active help, I am hampered in My work, even as
a human body is handicapped by the ineffective
operation of any particular member, however
small or insignificant. Thou canst not lie idle
without hindering the ministry of the Church
as a corporate body. Yea, thou canst not move
independently of My Spirit without causing
damage to the harmonious working of the whole;
for by My Spirit is oneness of thought and of
action produced. Lie not dormant. Be not sloth-
ful, neither allow thyself to sleep. . . .

Lo, I am with thee, and I will help thee. Be
not discouraged, neither weary of heart, for he
reapeth who faints not.

## As Rains of Refreshing

*Yea, brother, let me have joy of thee in the
Lord: refresh my bowels in the Lord.*

PHILEMON 20

As rains of refreshing, O Lord,
  So pour out Thy Spirit upon our waiting
hearts.
  As showers upon new-mown hay,
  O send Thy Spirit upon our thirsty souls.
  For upon Thee, O God, do we wait.
  Satisfy our hungering souls with Thine
abundance.
  Yea, fill Thou our longing hearts with Thy
fulness.
  For in Thy presence is fulness of Joy;
  At Thy right hand are eternal pleasures.

# Head into the Wind

*He maketh the storm a calm,*
*so that the waves thereof are still.*

PSALM 107:29

O My beloved, be not anxious concerning tomorrow. Thou shalt encounter nothing of which I am not already cognizant. My mercy is concealed within every storm cloud. My grace flows beneath every cross-current. My wisdom has conceived a solution to every perplexity. . . .

The storm is not a thing to fear but rather to welcome. Ye shall learn to head into the wind with sheer delight as soon as ye have made the discovery that in the time of stress and strain, ye have the clearest revelations of Myself.

Was it not true of the disciples? Looking out across the raging waters, what did they see? Was it not Jesus? Jesus—coming unto them! To have had this happen only once, would have been worth weathering many storms.

# Head into the Wind

## PART 2

*If we believe not, yet he abideth faithful:
he cannot deny himself.*

2 TIMOTHY 2:13

In the midst of the multi-heated fiery furnace, what saw the three Hebrew lads? Was it not the living form of Jesus Christ Himself having come to join company with them? Yea, He shone so bright to them that His brilliance obliterated the sight of the flames! . . .

Ye need never fear as to whether I will be faithful to thee, for if I have never failed anyone else, why would I fail thee? Ye have an innumerable company of spectators cheering thee from the ramparts of heaven, reminding you of what I did for them, and encouraging you that the struggle is not interminable, but surprisingly soon it shall end in victory for you also—if ye endure faithful.

# Head into the Wind
## PART 3

*Humble yourselves in the sight of the Lord,
and he shall lift you up.*

JAMES 4:10

Miracles burst forth out of the moist, cold soil of human tragedy. Moist with tears, and cold with hopelessness. I never get a chance to do miracles for you when you are occupied with self-realization—while ye are entertaining ideas about what wonderful thing I am going to make out of you. I do not use you for material for miracles; I make miracles out of My own Being. I allow you to watch Me after ye thoroughly understand that it is I who am supernatural, not you.

You do not have to be other than what I created you: human. You are only obligated to do that for which I created you: glorify Me. Stand back! Let God be God. Let man be man....

You need only stay humble.

# The Mind of God

*And the peace of God, which passeth all understanding, shall keep your hearts and minds through Christ Jesus.*

PHILIPPIANS 4:7

O My child, give Me your mind. I shall keep it in perfect tranquility. Give Me your thoughts. I will keep them in peace. If ye allow other people to do thy thinking for thee, thou shalt be distressed. If ye try to do it for thyself, ye may be in error through limited knowledge or misinformation. But let the mind of Christ be in you. . . .

As ye draw upon My Spirit for physical strength, so draw upon My Mind for wisdom and understanding and peace of mind. Make this a habit in thy life and thou shalt be astounded at the results, the accomplishments, it will bring. Rather than being motivated by impulse, ye shall be directed by Divine Intelligence.

# The Mind of God

## PART 2

*If any of you lack wisdom, let him ask of God, that giveth to all men liberally, and upbraideth not; and it shall be given him.*

JAMES 1:5

Ye shall be unafraid before the face of every man, for wisdom is power. Ye shall be unashamed to speak, for ye shall know that the words ye speak are not your own, but His Who has sent thee and made thee His messenger. Yes, you shall be able to testify as did Jesus: the words that I speak, I speak not of myself, but they are the words given me by the Father. . . .

Amazing things await thee. . . . The mind of God is fathomless. Who can ponder the smallest fraction of the intelligence of the Creator? It is all at thy disposal—a great repository upon which ye may freely draw. Draw, then, for truly "the well is deep."

# I Shall Rejoice in My People

*The LORD thy God in the midst of thee*
*is mighty; he will save, he will rejoice*
*over thee with joy; he will rest in his*
*love, he will joy over thee with singing.*

ZEPHANIAH 3:17

I will break through the locked gates as a flow of flaming lava.

I will not withhold My power and My glory from any seeking heart.

They who desire Me, I will surely reward: I will not fail.

I will fill every longing heart and satisfy every craving soul.

My grace will I pour out as a tumbling waterfall.

I shall be glorified, and I shall be magnified, and I shall rejoice in My people, in that day when they yield themselves fully and freely to Me: yea, when they give themselves utterly to Me and cut loose from all beside.

Then shall I cast My love about them as a cloak, and I shall whisper My words in their ears.

# Walk Ye in It

*He that putteth his trust in me shall possess
the land, and shall inherit my holy mountain.*

ISAIAH 57:13

Behold, I say unto thee,
This is the way. Walk ye in it.

Lo, I am the way.

Walk in Me.

I am the truth. Believe Me (trust in Me).

I am the Life. Live in Me, and share My life
with others.

For thou knowest not what I do now, but thou
shalt know hereafter.

(Now we see in a glass darkly, but then,
face to face. Now our grasp of the ways of God
is incomplete, but as we move on, we come to
understand what He has been endeavoring to
do in our lives.)

# Jewels

*Blessed is the man that endureth temptation:*
*for when he is tried, he shall receive the*
*crown of life, which the Lord hath*
*promised to them that love him.*

JAMES 1:12

I have betrothed thee unto Myself. Yea, I have given thee a special token of our relationship and our future union, for I have sealed thee with My precious Holy Spirit; and ye shall be Mine, saith the Lord, in that day when I make up My jewels, and ye shall be as a diadem upon My brow, yea, My crowning glory.

For I shall reign over kings and nations and peoples, yea, I shall be ruler over all the earth; but ye shall have a special place of honor, for thou art My prize possession. As it is written, having shared My agony, ye shall that day share My glory; having born for Me the cross, ye shall then share with Me the throne.

# Jewels

## PART 2

*And when the chief Shepherd shall
appear, ye shall receive a crown
of glory that fadeth not away.*

1 PETER 5:4

Rejoice now, that ye have been chosen out and counted worthy to suffer for My sake. We share one common destiny, and we walk one single path. At this present time, it may hold sorrow and isolation; but cheer thine heart with the raptures that lie ahead. Some live now in the revelries and riches of this present world who shall that day be mourners and paupers. Will ye exchange places? Would ye desert Me now and be rejected then? Would ye ignore Me now, and be in that day rejected by Me?

Nay, ye would not! Rather, ye will do as Paul: ye will glory in the midst of suffering and affliction, because ye know these things shall in that day be counter-balanced by an exceedingly greater portion of joy (weight of glory).

# Fortitude

*Study to shew thyself approved unto God,
a workman that needeth not to be ashamed,
rightly dividing the word of truth.*

2 TIMOTHY 2:15

In a multitude of testings, thou shalt learn courage. It matters not the price ye pay, but at any cost ye must obtain strength of character and the fortitude to endure. I would build thy resources until ye be able to carry unusually heavy loads and withstand intense pressures.

Ye shall thus become an ambassador of the Kingdom of Heaven to whom I can assign critical missions, being confident that ye are equipped to fulfill them.

It shall be in vain if ye anticipate resting in a comfortable place. Zion is already filled with those who are at ease. No, ye shall find thyself put in a place of training and discipline, so that when the moments of crisis come ye shall not become faint-hearted, and ye shall not be the victim of unwonted fear.

# On Doing the Father's Work

*But I have greater witness than that of John:*
*for the works which the Father hath given*
*me to finish, the same works that I do, bear*
*witness of me, that the Father hath sent me.*

JOHN 5:36

Behold, I say unto thee, there is a day coming when ye shall regret thy lethargy and ye shall say, "Why have we left the vineyard of the Lord uncared for?" . . .

Jesus Himself was directed by the Father in all that He said and did. Dare ye live according to the dictates of thine own carnal heart and puny human understanding?

Lo, I have fashioned thee for better things. Fail Me not, but place thy life under My divine control, and learn to live in the full blessing of My highest will.

I will strengthen thee and comfort thee and will lead thee by the hand.

# Find Solitude

*When thou prayest, enter into thy closet,*
*and when thou hast shut thy door, pray*
*to thy Father which is in secret; and*
*thy Father which seeth in secret*
*shall reward thee openly.*

MATTHEW 6:6

There is no blessing I would withhold from them that walk in obedience to Me—who follow when I call, and who respond when I speak unto them. They are near to My heart and precious in My sight who have eyes to discern My purpose and ears that listen to My direction.

Be not intent upon great accomplishments. By what standards do ye judge the importance of a matter? It was a relatively small thing that Hannah prayed for a son, but what great things I accomplished through Samuel! It may have seemed incidental that Simeon and Anna perceived the Christchild and prophesied over Him; but it was to Me a word worthy to be recorded in Holy Scripture and preserved forever.

# Find Solitude

## PART 2

*But the Lord is in his holy temple:*
*let all the earth keep silence before him.*

HABAKKUK 2:20

Nay, ye cannot ascertain the ways of God amidst the pathways of men. Ye may feel the wind as I pass, and yet see only the swirling dust. The earthly beclouds the heavenly. The voices of men drown the voice of God. Only in much solitude can ye begin to sift away the chaff and come at last to the golden grains of truth.

The World will confuse thee. Silence will speak more to thee in a day than the world of voices can teach thee in a lifetime. Find it. Find solitude—and having discovered her riches, bind her to thy heart.

# Renew Thy Vows

*Behold, the former things are come to pass,*
*and new things do I declare: before they*
*spring forth I tell you of them.*

<small>ISAIAH 42:9</small>

Renew thy vows, and I will revive thy ministry. There is a life ahead for thee into which ye could not have entered before. There is a work ready for thee, and I have prepared thee for it. It is too wonderful to miss. It shall be silent but powerful.

I shall cause the veil to drop, and ye shall enter a new area of experience. Ye shall be given a knowledge in My Spirit that is not to be found in books. I shall share with thee My thoughts, and who can tell the sum of them? Ye shall partake of the Mind of Christ and of the Holy Spirit of God. His eyes go throughout the whole earth seeking out the thoughts and intents of the hearts of men.

# The Road Is Steep

*Ye are holy unto the LORD; the vessels are holy also; and the silver and the gold are a freewill offering unto the LORD God of your fathers.*

EZRA 8:28

Ye are a chosen vessel unto Me, saith the Lord; be not filled with filthy lucre. Be not defiled with the lusts of the flesh and tarnished with the pride of life. Be ye wholesome, humble, simple; for simplicity and a spirit of humility befit one who is a servant of the Lord.

Pride lifteth up. It exalteth self rather than Christ. Humility bringeth down to the level of service, and ye are not to be worshipped, but to serve.

Ye are My treasure. I delight in you when, and only when, ye are fully yielded to Me with no thoughts of personal ambition or achievement.

# The Road Is Steep
## PART 2

*Go thou near, and hear all that the L*ORD *our God shall say: and speak thou unto us all that the L*ORD *our God shall speak unto thee; and we will hear it, and do it.*

DEUTERONOMY 5:27

*If ye wish* for anything, wish for more of My personal nearness. If ye long after anything, long after more of My righteousness and more of My love. For I will not occupy second place, and My Spirit will take leave of an impure vessel. Even as sin hath no place in heaven, just so, I will not dwell in peace in a heart that harbors evil. . . .

Holiness is arrived at by no low road. The road to holiness is narrow and steep and exceedingly lonely. There is no other road. "It is the way the Master went, Shall not His servants tread it still?"

# I Will Use, but Not Destroy You

*So shall my word be that goeth forth out of my mouth: it shall not return unto me void, but it shall accomplish that which I please, and it shall prosper in the thing whereto I sent it.*

ISAIAH 55:11

Be not overcharged with the cares of everyday living, and let not thine energies be consumed by the humdrum tasks. Such as is needful, ye must do, but if ye put the ministry of the Kingdom in first place, My strength shall be yours for the other tasks, and time shall be given thee for both.

Ye do not need to respond to every call. Learn to discern when I would use you, and when I would have the other individual lean wholly upon Me. . . .

I will honor My Word, and I will honor them that give to My Word the sacred preeminence which it deserves.

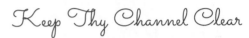

## Keep Thy Channel Clear

*But my God shall supply all
your need according to his
riches in glory by Christ Jesus.*

PHILIPPIANS 4:19

O My daughter, shall I speak unto thee as one whose voice is lost in the noise of crashing surf, or as one who calls in vain in the midst of a deep forest, where there is no ear to hear nor voice to respond? Will ye be as an instrument with broken strings from which the musician can bring forth no music?

Nay, I would have you to be as the waterfall whose sound is continuous, and as a great river whose flow is not interrupted. Ye shall not sing for a time and then be silent for a season. Ye shall not praise for a day, and then revert to the current topics of everyday life.

Ye shall never exhaust My supply.

# Keep Thy Channel Clear
## PART 2

*He that believeth on me, as the*
*scripture hath said, out of his belly*
*shall flow rivers of living* water.

JOHN 7:38

*I will bring* My love and My life to thee. . . . The more often ye come to Me to draw of this water of Life, the more shall thy life be enriched in wisdom—yes, but also in many other ways. . . . Ye need to keep thy channel straight and clear, that My blessing be not hindered in flowing through thee, and that the waters may be kept pure. . . .

I was in the still small voice. I Myself am the direct source and the only source of eternal life. Every other well is dry. Every other pursuit is vain.

But ye shall be a fountain flowing forth whose streams shall not fail, for I, the Lord thy God, dwell in the midst of thee.

# Speak the Truth

*Sanctify them through
thy truth: thy word is truth.*

JOHN 17:17

Lo, I say unto thee, be not intimidated by anyone, but speak forth My Word, even as I give it unto thee. Ye have written freely and fearlessly. Now speak in the same way. Thy spoken word must be brought into conformity with the work I have done within thee. This ye need for your own personal sense of unity. This ye need for your own strength. For the house divided against itself cannot stand; neither can ye so long as ye bear one testimony in thine heart and another with thy lips. . . .

Let the life and witness of Jesus Christ be your guide. . . .

Set not out upon a mission to convert the world to your convictions, but rather to hold your own convictions inviolable against the forces of the opposition. I will be with thee, and will keep thy mouth. Trust Me.

# Come Away, My Beloved

*My beloved spake, and said unto me, Rise up,*
*my love, my fair one, and come away.*

SONG OF SOLOMON 2:10

*I go before* you. Yea, I shall engineer circumstances on thy behalf. I am thy husband, and I will protect thee and care for thee, and make full provision for thee....

For man is experiencing a new awakening, and he is searching for My Truth more than ever, and I must speak through My prophets; and if they be not separated unto Me, how can I instruct them? Yea, I shall nourish thee by the brook as I nourished Elijah; and I shall speak to thee out of the bush as I spoke to Moses, and reveal My glory on the hillside as I did to the shepherds.

COME AWAY, MY BELOVED, and be as the doe upon the mountains; yea, we shall go down together to the gardens.

# Take the Glory with Thee

*He brought me forth also into a large place;*
*he delivered me, because he delighted in me.*

PSALM 18:19

Behold, I have brought thee out of a dark and solitary land. I have given thee to drink out of My hand. We have held sweet counsel together; for I have not called thee servant, but I have called thee friend. Yea, and I delight in thy companionship. For I have seen thy devotion, and I have observed with pleasure thy thoughtfulness of those less-fortunate ones who have crossed thy path.

For when thou hast encouraged the weary, and when thou hast prayed with the sick, and when thou hast lent help to the needy, comfort to the sorrowing, understanding to the distressed, I count it as unto Myself, for I know that except for thy deep love for Me, thou wouldst not make this kind of sacrifice.

# Take the Glory with Thee
## PART 2

*And the sight of the glory of the LORD was*
*like devouring fire on the top of the mount*
*in the eyes of the children of Israel.*

EXODUS 24:17

For if a man love God, truly he will love his brother likewise. Yea, and he will yet go beyond this, for he will show kindness and feel concern for the needs of even his enemies, and be moved with compassion to minister aid.

Said I not that we must needs go into the valley together? I have given the mountaintop of the enjoyment of My fellowship to prepare thee for the ministry in the valley of service. TAKE THE GLORY OF THE MOUNTAINTOP WITH THEE, yea, My presence, My light, My love. This is not the valley of personal darkness: this is the valley where walk those who need the touch of blessing thou canst bring.

# Take the Glory with Thee
## PART 3

*Who now rejoice in my sufferings for you,*
*and fill up that which is behind of the*
*afflictions of Christ in my flesh for his*
*body's sake, which is the church.*

COLOSSIANS 1:24

And I am with thee, yea, more so than in any other kind of valley; for in this we are *one* in a very special way. For the Son of Man came to seek and to save that which was lost; to seek that which was lost, and to lift that which was fallen, and to heal that which was bruised. . . .

So yield thyself to the movings of the Spirit in thy heart, and minister as I arrange thy contacts, nor set about to make thine own choices. Leave the planning to the Head. This is My work. Let each abide in his place, yielding completely to My Spirit, nourished by My love, and ministering in self-sacrifice.

## Listen to the Silence

*Hope and quietly wait for*
*the salvation of the LORD.*
LAMENTATIONS 3:26

You are in My hands. You are not keeping yourself; I am keeping you. If I choose to hide you away, it is for a purpose. If I wish to give you a time of rest, it is for thine own good. Nothing is amiss that is in My will. Do not think that it will be as times in the past. I have deeper lessons to teach you. How invaluable have you found the truths to be which I have taught you in your "Arabia years." Arabia was not the only solitary period in the life of St. Paul. Indeed, it was rather insignificant in comparison to the later prison day experiences.

One does not write what has already been written. One writes out of the storehouse of fresh revelation and his own personal knowledge gained through the painful experiences of growth.

# Listen to the Silence
## PART 2

*Be still, and know that I am God.*
PSALM 46:10

*I would spare* you if I could do so in love; but this kind of protecting love would be false, and would rob you of much treasure. I only love you truly as I give you My best. My best cannot come to you without pain, even as it could not come to the Lord Jesus without pain. . . . The kingdom of Satan must likewise be opposed by a stronger force if ye hope to see it fall.

I want to make you strong. I want you to be a Devastator. I have brought you to this place. Make the most of it. Drink in the silence. Seek solitude. LISTEN TO THE SILENCE. It will teach you. It will build strength. Let others share it with you. It is priceless. It is little to be found elsewhere.

# A More Glorious Way

*The letter killeth, but the spirit giveth life.*
2 CORINTHIANS 3:6

*I say unto* thee that I have a deeper revelation of this truth to give unto thee if ye can receive it. For the Spirit operateth in a different realm than the Word. The Word dealeth with thee on the plane of thine everyday living. It governs thy conduct in daily affairs. It guideth thee into the knowledge of the doctrines of God, the understanding of the divine will, and instructs thee in the walk of the Christian.

But in the Spirit, there is a life awaiting thee that would draw thee out beyond the confines of the natural world. The Spirit of God operate in the realm of the supernatural and the infinite.

Do not hold back in wonder and disbelief. Accept My life in the Spirit *as it is.*

# A More Glorious Way
## PART 2

*I will instruct thee and teach thee
in the way which thou shalt go.*

PSALM 32:8

𝒪nly the heart that is melted in devotion is pliable in My hand. Only the mind that is open to the Spirit can receive divine revelation.

Labor not to be wise but to be yielded, and in thine attitude of submission to My Spirit I will instruct thee in My truth. There shall be death and there shall be a glorious resurrection. For the letter shall convict of sin and prune away the old carnal nature, and the Spirit shall bring forth within thee a life that shall never die. It shall have faculties of perception not to be compared with the physical senses; for the mind of the Spirit is the Mind of Christ.

It shall increase and develop as ye move on into God, and ye shall leave behind the graveclothes of religious intellectualism and discover a more glorious way.

# I Want to Do a Beautiful Work

*Wherefore also it is contained in the scripture, Behold, I lay in Sion a chief corner stone, elect, precious: and he that believeth on him shall not be confounded.*

1 PETER 2:6

Ye are Mine, saith the Lord. Ye are not your own. With a very great price have I purchased thee unto Myself. I am not dismayed that ye do not comprehend, but I say unto thee, that if ye will harken unto Me, I will reveal to thee more fully so that ye may know more clearly how vital you are in My purpose. There is work to be done and I need you as a vessel through which to work. Not a vassal, but a vessel. I want to do a beautiful work. . . .

What a blessed reward I have in store! Yes, in store for *you*, if you are able to let Me use you in the way which I desire to do.

# The Secret of Silence

*Ye shall walk in all the ways which the L<small>ORD</small>
your God hath commanded you, that ye may
live, and that it may be well with you, and
that ye may prolong your days in the land
which ye shall possess.*

<small>DEUTERONOMY 5:33</small>

*If ye will* accept My love and My approval, ye
shall be given courage to face thy sins and faults
and deal with them with more decisiveness. The
more ye find of the truth about thine own self,
the more ye shall be set free. . .free of improper
evaluations of thy worth and false pride that
seeks to cover recognized flaws.

I want your life and character and personality to be as beautiful and lovely as I visualized
it to be when I created you. . . . *Live close to Me*,
and let Me re-mold and re-create until I see in
thee the image of all I want thee to be.

# The Secret of Silence
## PART 2

*He will teach us of his ways, and we will walk
in his paths: for the law shall go forth of Zion,
and the word of the LORD from Jerusalem.*

MICAH 4:2

*I love thee,* My child—My very dear and special child. Through thy childhood years I walked very close to thee, and in thy childlike way ye were very conscious of My presence and reality. Ye have made an arduous journey. Ye have climbed many a mountain that ye could easily have walked around. Ye have not chosen the pleasant path nor sought joys though they were readily accessible. . . .

I will rebuild your strength—not to work again in foolish frenzy, but just for the sake of making you strong and well. To Me this is an end in itself. Make it your aim and join with Me wholeheartedly in the project. "Many joys are waiting yet."

# The Love Covenant

*When the enemy shall come in like
a flood, the Spirit of the LORD shall
lift up a standard against him.*

ISAIAH 59:19

My children, there is no good thing that I would withhold from thee. I have not left you to fend for yourselves nor to make your way by your own devices. I am the Lord, thy God. I am thy provider and thy defender. I care for thee with a deep and tender love. I am all-wise and all-powerful, and will be thy defense against every onslaught of the enemy.

Anticipate My help. I will not fail thee. Look down at the path before thee. Thou shalt see the print of My feet, for as scripture saith, I go before thee, and I make the path ready for thee as ye follow.

It is a joy to My heart when My children rely upon Me.

# The Love Covenant

## PART 2

*Abide in me, and I in you. As the branch
cannot bear fruit of itself, except it abide in the
vine; no more can ye, except ye abide in me.*

JOHN 15:4

*I delight in* working things out for thee, but I
delight even more in *thee thyself* than in anything I do to help thee. Even so, I want *you* to
delight in *Me* just for *Myself*, rather than in
anything ye do for Me.

Service is the salvage of love. It is like the
twelve baskets of bread that were left over. The
bread partaken of was like fellowship mutually
given; and the excess and overflow were a sym-
bol of service. I do not expect thee to give to
others until ye have first thyself been a partaker.
I will provide you with plentiful supply to GIVE if
ye first come to RECEIVE for thine own needs.

## The Gift of Forgiveness

*For God so loved the world, that
he gave his only begotten Son, that
whosoever believeth in him should
not perish, but have everlasting life.*

JOHN 3:16

*I want to* give you a new gift. I want you to
see all people as being under the sacrifice of the
blood of Christ.

He has died for all. His forgiveness encom-
passeth all. Tell them. It is the Good News. They
will accept it even as they have received eagerly
and joyfully the message of My *love*. It is the
confidence in thine own heart that will engender
faith to receive within the hearts of others.

Freely forgive all, even as ye have freely loved
all. Those to whom ye extend My forgiveness
shall come to experience it for themselves even
as ye would extend a helping hand to lift another
across a brook.

# The Gift of Forgiveness
## PART 2

*In whom we have redemption through
his blood, the forgiveness of sins,
according to the riches of his grace.*

EPHESIANS 1:7

Thou wilt find the Christ Himself standing beside thee, and thou shalt see His smile. . . .

I am bringing you into a new ministry. The former shall be enriched and made fuller and more meaningful. I am not undoing anything. I am adding to. I shall be enriching thine own soul and effecting thy sanctification.

Ye have need of many graces as well as many gifts. The *graces* of thy soul accompany thee into the next life, whereas the *gifts* are left behind. For this reason the health of thine own soul is of more importance to thyself than the fulness of thy ministry. But each time ye launch out into a new ministry ye bring new life and strength and health-building forces into operation within thine own soul.

# The Eye of the Spirit

*Neither shall one thrust another; they shall
walk every one in his path: and when they fall
upon the sword, they shall not be wounded.*

JOEL 2:8

The limitations of thy natural vision shall be
no handicap. The Spirit is not detained by the
flesh. . . . Naught shall be required of thee but
obedience. Thou shalt follow the call of the
Spirit and not search for the path; for the way
shall be laid down before thee even as ye tread.
Wherever ye stop, there shall the path stop also.
Whenever ye walk in faith, the way shall be made
clear before thee.

Be as a young child and step out in confidence,
knowing that with thy hand in Mine ye shall be
always safe and blessings shall attend thee.

# With Winged Feet

*Then shalt thou walk in thy way safely,*
*and thy foot shall not stumble.*

PROVERBS 3:23

I am aware of thy needs and shall provide in abundance, but it is for My glory and My honor, and I shall have the praise.

Thou shalt tread lightly and not allow thy feet to be ensnared in the net of undue concern for the things about thee. They are Mine, saith the Lord, even as all things are Mine, and you yourselves are Mine; and I am more interested in you than in things. Likewise, I want you to be occupied with Me rather than with My gifts. I will take care of both them and thyself. Is it not a small thing for me to do?

Be alert to My voice. Let not thine ear lose its keenness of listening. Be devoted to Me with thy whole heart, and put all that is about thee into My keeping.

# With Winged Feet
## PART 2

*For the LORD shall be thy confidence, and
shall keep thy foot from being taken.*

PROVERBS 3:26

Thou shalt evidence My love and reality to those
who have not as yet experienced My nearness
and fellowship in the way in which you have
known Me.

I have need of thee as a light to shine in
dark places. I have not called thee by some fickle
whim. As it is written, How shall the message go
out without a messenger? I have made thee My
messenger. Thou shalt go with winged feet. Thou
shalt not allow thy foot to be bogged down in
the mire of earthly cares and riches.

Thou shalt discharge thy duties with dispatch
and shalt deal in wisdom with each responsibility; but thine heart shall rest in My hand. Thy
thoughts shall return to Me as the needle to the
pole and as the bird to its nest.

# The Secret

*For then shalt thou lift up thy
face without spot; yea, thou shalt
be stedfast, and shalt not fear.*

JOB 11:15

There's a little word that changes
　　Darkest skies to brightest blue;
There's a little word that brings the
　　Sunlight bravely shining through.
ever mind the things about you;
　　Never mind if others frown—
Lift your face to God and praise Him,
　　And the blessings will come down!
Praise is mightier than an army
　　With its banners all unfurled;
Praise will win the victory sooner
　　Than all the powers of this world.
For the God who ruleth all things,
　　And the God who longs to bless
Waiteth only till He heareth thee
　　Thy love to Him confess.

# The Secret

## PART 2

*Bow thy heavens, O LORD, and come down:*
*touch the mountains, and they shall smoke.*

PSALM 144:5

Beg Him not for any blessing; Tire Him not
to spell thy need.

This He knoweth e'er thou speak it; Stay Him
not to beg and plead.

Lift thy face and sing it heav'nward,

From the deeps within thy soul; Let His
praises fill thy being,

Let the shout of rapture roll.

Ah! The rest will come quite easy—E'er thou
thinkest, 'twill be done.

Thou wilt know PRAISE is the answer.

Thou wilt find the vict'ry won.

Blessed, holy, wondrous Jesus, Heav'n in
Thee to me is come!

# Delight Thyself in Me

*Be careful for nothing; but in every thing by*
*prayer and supplication with thanksgiving*
*let your requests be made known unto God.*

PHILIPPIANS 4:6

My child, be not anxious concerning the growth of thy soul. Leave it with Me. Have I not said that the lilies grow without taking thought of themselves? Even so must ye, both in the natural and in the spiritual.

To be sure, there are conditions that must be met in order to insure healthy, normal development; however, these conditions are not created by anxiety, but anxiety militates against them.

Be occupied with acquainting thyself with My character and My person. Revel in My fellowship. Thy very association with Me, if it be sufficiently consistent, will bring about changes in thine own personality that will be a surprise to thee when discovered, even as thou hast so often experienced the joy of finding a new bloom on a cherished plant.

# Delight Thyself in Me
## PART 2

*He trusted on the LORD that he would*
*deliver him: let him deliver him,*
*seeing he delighted in him.*

PSALM 22:8

Turn thy face toward Me, and leave to Me the responsibility of probing thy soul. I am the Master Surgeon. I am skilled in all the cures of the soul as well as those of the body. Let Me care for thy health.

*Delight thyself in Me*, and I shall bring about that which ye desire to see in thy character and personality. Feed upon My Word. It is there that ye shall come to a clearer understanding of My Person. Only as ye know Me can ye come to be more like Me.

. . .[M]an taketh to himself a measure of the mannerisms and ideologies of these other persons. So shall it be likewise to those who spend much time in My company.

Silently, and without conscious effort, thou shalt be changed.

# Relinquish Thy Will

*For whom the Lord loveth he chasteneth,*
*and scourgeth every son whom he receiveth.*

HEBREWS 12:6

My heart is grieved by thine independence. How would Joseph have felt if his father and family had remained at home, starving in the famine, when he had invited them to share the bountiful stores which he had at his disposal and desired to share freely with them (Genesis 45)?

Would he not have grieved far more deeply than over the unjust actions of his brothers who hated him? For to be rebuffed by a loved one causeth pain not to be compared with the cruelties inflicted by an enemy. So thine indifference and unresponsiveness to My call bringeth anguish to My soul, yea, deeper grief than the crimes of the reprobate sinner. For My rod have I laid upon the sinner, but Mine hand have I laid upon thee.

# Relinquish Thy Will

## PART 2

*When they had brought their ships to land,
they forsook all, and followed him.*

LUKE 5:11

And I have put Mine arm about thee to draw thee closer, but ye have been impatient and irritable as though I sought to interfere with thy liberty. Lo, I am able to give thee greater liberty than thou shalt ever find by seeking to be independent of Me. I seek not to interfere with thy happiness, but I do require that thou relinquish thy will; for I cannot bless thee as I desire to do until thy will is yielded up and thou accept Mine in exchange.

As thou lovest Me, thou acceptest My will as thine own, and the calibre and extent of thy love for Me may be accurately measured by the degree to which thou hast accepted My will with a peaceful heart.

# I Control the Winds

*The men marvelled, saying, What manner
of man is this, that even the winds
and the sea obey him!*

MATTHEW 8:27

Thy times are in My hand. Thy way is open before Me, and I have all in My control. Never doubt My care. Never question My dealings.

Ye shall know that I am leading thee by the narrowness of the way. Yea, it is ofttimes a difficult and a precipitous path; but I would assure thee of My hand of protection. Do not think it strange that I bring you by this route, for I say unto thee that there is a raucous crowd on the other road, and there is an abundance of places of entertainment and of places to eat and to drink.

I am not taking you that way, because in the solitary and the steep and narrow way I shall have opportunity to deal with thee and to teach thee.

# I Control the Winds

## PART 2

*He said unto them, Where is your faith?*
*And they being afraid wondered, saying*
*one to another, What manner of man is*
*this! for he commandeth even the winds*
*and water, and they obey him.*

LUKE 8:25

Ye shall be blessed and shall learn to praise Me with uncontrollable joy.

I cannot produce saints and shape My character and image within you by allowing you full and unrestricted liberty. There can be nothing profitable for you in the matter of the growth of thy soul if ye go the way of abandon.

Put thy life in My hands, and it shall be for thee a place of peace and of spiritual comfort. So long as ye abide in this place, I shall control the rains that fall upon thee and the winds that blow. So long as ye are in My hands, ye are in a garrison the walls of which no enemy shall scale.

# Allow Me Ingress to Thy Heart

*And I will give thee the treasures of darkness,*
*and hidden riches of secret places.*

ISAIAH 45:3

O My people, be watchful and be much in prayer. I cannot mold thee and shape thee and perfect thee unless ye provide Me the opportunity to do so. I can only minister to the needs of thy soul as ye allow Me ingress to the hidden places of thy heart.

Ye can set up a barrier against Me to prevent My entrance, and I will not interfere. Open wide thy being to Me in the intimacy of prayer, and then, and only then, shall I take the liberty to correct thee and show thee thy faults.

I long to do this for thee, because I desire to make thee into a closer resemblance to My divine nature. I would change thy human frailties to My strength. I would take thy resentments, and give thee My grace.

# Allow Me Ingress to Thy Heart

## PART 2

*Christi in you, the hope of glory.*

COLOSSIANS 1:27

*I am thy* God, and I rule the universe and keep it operating by My will. But to thee I have given this most sacred thing: *thy will.* I have given thee so much freedom that ye may even exercise that will against Me, if ye choose to do so.

Yield to Me, and I will shape and form thy soul to conform to My pattern of beauty and holiness. Much that is considered as holiness by men's standards is distortion in My eyes. Ye are not prepared to judge thine own life, neither to draw a pattern for piety.

Fix thine heart upon Me, and as ye behold My glory, ye shall be changed, and My own likeness shall be formed within thee.

# Come into the Secret Chambers of Communion

*The true worshippers shall worship the Father in spirit and in truth: for the Father seeketh such to worship him.*

JOHN 4:23

O My beloved, My desire is toward thee. Yea, My heart longeth after thee. Grieve Me not by thine indifference. For I would gather thee; but ye heed Me not. I would embrace thee and caress thee; but ye are impatient to be away. Ye cannot please Me thus.

For I have called thee to come into the secret chambers of solitary communion. They are dark; but the comfort of My Person is there. Out of darkness cometh great treasure.

The dazzle and glitter of public life is attractive to the eye of the carnal man; but I would closet you away in the secret places of humility and discipline of soul, denying the things that pertain to the outward man in order to perfect the inner life and enrich thy knowledge of Myself.

# I Seek to Lift Thy Load

*For my yoke is easy, and my burden is light.*

MATTHEW 11:30

Ye need Me in the early hours for direction and guidance and for my blessing upon thy heart. Ye need Me at the end of the day to commit into My hands the day's happenings—both to free thyself of the burdens and to give them over into My hands that I may continue to work things out. And ye need Me more than ever in the busy hours, in the activities and responsibilities, that I may give thee My grace and My tranquility and My wisdom.

I do not ask you to take time for Me with the intention of placing a burden upon thee in requiring thee to do so. Rather than adding a requirement, I seek to lift thy load. Rather than burdening thee with a devotional obligation, I desire to take from thee the tensions of life.

## Heart-Purity

*Create in me a clean heart, O God;*
*and renew a right spirit within me.*
PSALM 51:10

O My children, 'tis not in thy grieving over thy sins that they are forgiven. Lo, I say unto thee that My forgiveness is in constant operation and ye need only accept it. The cleansing of thy heart and the restoration of thy joy depends upon thy full confession and willingness to repent and to renounce thy sin. It is in this area that ye need to exercise thy soul toward the achievement of heart-purity, and until this work is accomplished (and maintained) ye shall not have inner peace.

This unrest and conflict that ye suffer is not caused by My attitude toward thee but by thine attitude toward thyself. Ye know that all is not well within. Ye would do well to seek My face in repentance until all that distresses thee is yielded up to Me.

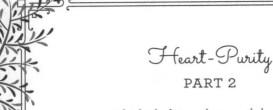

# Heart-Purity

## PART 2

*The little foxes, that spoil the vines:
for our vines have tender grapes.*

SONG OF SOLOMON 2:15

No true saint who seeketh to please Me escapes the onslaughts of the devil. He is a prime target who sets himself to a life of prayer. Ye need the armor if ye decide to go out to battle. For in serving Me, ye anger the enemy and he will not allow thee to gain ground spiritually without seeking to hurl against thee his poisoned arrows of doubts and accusations.

Resist him, as scripture admonishes thee. He is not courageous, but he is sly, and he is not easily discouraged. Ye can never escape his snare until ye recognize his activities and strike at the source.

Do not attack thy discouragement, but resist the one who would put it upon thee. Do not doubt My forgiveness, but close thine ears to the accuser.

# Thy Life Is as a Weaving

*For we are his workmanship, created
in Christ Jesus unto good works.*

EPHESIANS 2:10

My child, thy life is as a weaving. Beauty shall not come to thee by joy alone. Life may be tortuous at times, and the pathway rough. From fabrics of lovely silk and from cords of rougher materials, I fashion what pleaseth Me. Ye may never know why certain experiences come. It is enough that My hand brings them all.

My grace is limited in no way by sorrow and difficulty. Indeed, it shines like a strand of gold mixed in with the black of grief. My hand moveth with infinite love and I am creating a pattern of intricate beauty.

Be never dismayed. The end shall bring rejoicing for both thyself and Me. For ye are My workmanship, created in Christ, even in His mind before the worlds existed.

Doubt not, for My will *shall* be done.

# I Wait for Thee

*For man looketh on the outward appearance,
but the L*ORD *looketh on the heart.*

1 SAMUEL 16:7

With great love have I chosen thee and made thee Mine, saith the Lord. My heart is drawn out toward thee. . . .

I wait for thee to turn from everything else to Me alone. I want you to give Me all of yourself. I want the real you. The more you can bring to Me of your true self, the more I can give to you of My true self.

If ye come to Me with any kind of cloak over your soul, just to this extent ye hinder Me from fully opening My heart to you. I am neither disturbed by imperfections nor impressed with piety. People look upon the outward, but I am only concerned with the heart; for I know that whenever I can occupy the heart, all will be working toward perfection in the outer man.

# I Wait for Thee
## PART 2

*I stand at the door, and knock: if
any man hear my voice, and open
the door, I will come in to him.*

REVELATION 3:20

It is as though a guest came to a home and entered the inner sanctum, rather than coming by way of the outer gate. He would then not be mindful of the gate or the garden nor the exterior of the house. I come to thee via My Holy Spirit from depths within thy being that thou hast never seen.—Rooms of darkness.—Not dark because of sin necessarily, as ye think of sin; but dark because they have been kept closed.

Indeed, none but I have the key to open them. I not only have the power to open them, but the wisdom and the love; and I never confront thee with that which I do not give thee grace to meet.

## Enter the Flow

*The glory of the God of Israel came*
*from the way of the east: and his*
*voice was like a noise of many waters:*
*and the earth shined with his glory.*

EZEKIEL 43:2

It is the flowing lines of the sculptor's work that spell success. It is the flowing movement of the musical score that transforms mere notes to true song. It is the ministries of mother to child, either physical or spiritual, that contribute to the formation of the new personality and character. It is in the fulfillment of the joint responsibilities and services between husband and wife that love is nurtured and fulfillment experienced.

It is love *being* and love *doing*. Yea, it is love *loving*. Otherwise it is concept, not reality. It is the believer *worshipping*—otherwise it is empty religion, with all spiritual creativity lost, and if not found in time, destroyed.

# Enter the Flow

## PART 2

*Let the floods clap their hands:*
*let the hills be joyful together.*

PSALM 98:8

So the trees would say to thee, *Speak.* Speak to Me, speak of Me—for I am always speaking.

And the lake would say to thee, *Be still.* Be still before Me in communion, and be still at times even in the company of others, that ye may enjoy the lesson of the lake in mutual fellowship.

And *Move.* Find the channel of creativity within thy soul. I have made no man without it. Some have choked it with indifference; others have despised it in rebellion; others have ignored it in foolishness; others have twisted it in bitterness. But I stand ready to come to the assistance of any man or woman who sincerely endeavors to find his channel, to remove debris, to repair damage, or straighten the course, and most of all to enter the flow.

It is the flow of divine life.

# I Make No Provision for the Laggard

*And a stranger will they not follow,*
*but will flee from him: for they know*
*not the voice of strangers.*

JOHN 10:5

Ye have heard My voice and have known that
it is I Myself who have been ministering unto
thee. Ye have not followed the voice of a stranger
nor sought out strange paths. For this reason
have I set My love upon thee. I have put Mine
arm around thee, and with My wings have I
sheltered thee. Ye are the object of My special
attention and ye have received My special care.

I have given thee of My best because ye have
loved Me. I have drawn thee into My banquet-
ing hall because ye have hungered and thirsted
after the things of God. Yea, because ye have
longed for righteousness and true holiness I have
sought thee out to instruct thee and teach thee in
My laws and in My ways.

# I Make No Provision for the Laggard
## PART 2

*Thy word have I hid in mine heart,*
*that I might not sin against thee.*

PSALM 119:11

Listen to the voice of My Spirit within. It will never fail. It will never be silent. It will never mock thy cry. Thine hours of meditation shall be rich in the treasures of thy God, and His light shall guide thee.

It is no futile path in which I am leading you. It shall be laden with blessing and filled with surprises. Be not hesitant to follow. If ye lag behind, ye may find My footprints have become cold because I have gone on too far ahead. I charge you to keep pace with Me. I will not gauge My steps too wide for thee to follow. I will measure them to thine ability, but I make no provision for the laggard.

Follow close, and your reward shall be blessed.

# The Solitary Relationship

*For I have redeemed thee, I have
called thee by thy name; thou art mine.*

ISAIAH 43:1

The Lord hath dealt bountifully with thee;
yea, He hath blessed thee in abundance and
hath multiplied thy joys. He hath set thee in a
safe place; He hath made thee to dwell in the
mountain of His grace; He hath covered thee
with His mercies. Blessed be His name, for
He will surround thee with His presence and
satisfy thine heart with His love.

Be not dismayed, neither allow any anxiety to
find a nesting place in thy thoughts. For thou art
Mine, saith the Lord, and My hand shall protect
thee. I will allow no evil to come nigh thee.

Thou art My possession. I shall brook no
rivalry. Rebuke the enemy and he shall flee from
thee. Count upon My care: I cannot fail. He that
keepeth his confidence in Me shall never be
disappointed.

# The Solitary Relationship
## PART 2

*Ye shall walk in all the ways which the LORD
your God hath commanded you, that ye
may live, and that it may be well with you,
and that ye may prolong your days in
the land which ye shall possess.*

DEUTERONOMY 5:33

This is a solitary walk. This abiding place in Me is completely removed from the multitude; yea, it is a place to be shared with no other—not even thy dearest friend. This knowing Me in secret is an experience alien to the world. This union with Me is the source of thy life, of thy strength, of thy health and vitality. Nothing can substitute.

. . .Seek that place in Me where no other can intrude. Thou wilt find Me there, and in finding Me thus, ye shall discover all other lacks fulfilled; for in Me there is abundant Life, and with Me there are only joys, and this forever.

# Relax Not Thy Vigil

*Awake, awake; put on thy strength,*
*O Zion; put on thy beautiful garments,*
*O Jerusalem, the holy city: for henceforth*
*there shall no more come into thee the*
*uncircumcised and the unclean.*

ISAIAH 52:1

For My people, saith the Lord, lift up thy voice and weep aloud.

Yea, let thy cry be heard in the night.

In the stillness, rouse the sleeping.

Say ye to My people, Up, shake thyself from slumber. Lay aside thy garments of sleep. Gird thyself and put sandals on thy feet. Make haste.

Yea, flee to the rock of refuge lest in thy drowsiness, sleeping past the hour, thou waken at last to find thyself ensnared in the net of the enemy. For the powers of darkness are about thee on every side. Yea, he doth not rest in his scheming and plotting. For he desireth with an unholy, fiendish delight and with bitter, deliberate design, to destroy the godly and to break down the building of God.

# Relax Not Thy Vigil

## PART 2

*Be sober, be vigilant; because your adversary
the devil, as a roaring lion, walketh about,
seeking whom he may devour.*

1 PETER 5:8

But I have built My Church, and founded it upon the Rock, and the very gates of hell shall not prevail against it.

I would not that ye be unaware of [the enemy's] devices; but having calculated the strength of the opposing force thou shalt be moved to see thy need of greater power that ye be not overcome.

For My power is available to thee.

Yea, I will Myself fight for thee if thou put thy trust in Me. Only relax not thy vigil.

For they that stumble, stumble in the darkness, and they that slumber do so in the night.

Be thou not overtaken.

Fix thine eyes upon the Sun of Righteousness and He shall cause thee to walk in a path of light.

# According to Mine Eternal Purposes

*According to the eternal purpose which*
*he purposed in Christ Jesus our Lord:*
*In whom we have boldness and access*
*with confidence by the faith of him.*

EPHESIANS 3:11–12

Hold thou fast, for lo, I am with thee:
Stand thou still, for I am thy God.
Be thou quiet before Me,

For I have arranged all things for thee according to My good will, yea, according to Mine eternal purposes.

For I have purposes and plans and desires which reach far beyond thy present view.

Thou seest as it were the immediate situation, but My thoughts for thee, and My planning for thee embraces eternity. Yea, thou art in My hand.

Rest there, and leave all else to Me.

# Give Not Substitutes

*O taste and see that the LORD is good:*
*blessed is the man that trusteth in him.*

PSALM 34:8

My people are hungering for My Word, and when ye are gathered together, I would that ye feed them.

Give not inedible substitutes. Give the lovely bread of the words of Jesus. Yea, spread a feast, and enjoy the delicious and the rich meats of divine truth.

Why should ye hunger when such plenty is at hand? And why should ye be deprived of spiritual nourishment when a table is spread before thee?

Some of the foods may be strange to thee. Despise nothing that I offer thee. Thou needest it, else I would not provide it. Partake of it, even if it is strange to thy taste. Ye will soon come to relish it with delight, and even more so because it *is* a new experience for thee.

# Give Not Substitutes

## PART 2

*Yet the LORD hath not given you an*
*heart to perceive, and eyes to see,*
*and ears to hear, unto this day.*

DEUTERONOMY 29:4

Keep thy mind open, else how can ye grow? Fear not deception nor poison. So long as ye seek Me, ye shall be rewarded in finding *Me*. What ye *seek*, that shall ye *find*.

Ye shall not seek bread and find a stone. Ye shall not seek fish and find a scorpion. Ye need have no fear except the fear of a mis-directed quest. Let My Holy Spirit reign in the desires of thy heart, and ye shall be thus guarded from unworthy motives. Let Me keep thy motives free of fleshly lusts and channeled into the paths of righteousness.

Open thine eyes to all I show thee, and open thy mouth wide and let Me fill it as I have promised to do.

# Stay Beneath My Wing

*When thou passest through the waters, I will*
*be with thee; and through the rivers, they*
*shall not overflow thee: when thou walkest*
*through the fire, thou shalt not be burned;*
*neither shall the flame kindle upon thee.*

ISAIAH 43:2

Yea, I shall bring My will to pass, and man shall know that his will is as a broken straw when pitted against the Almighty.

But My people shall know the protection of their God. Because their heart is stayed upon Jehovah, therefore shall I keep them in My pavilion and shelter them until the calamity be overpassed.

If I removed thee from the scene, ye would have no testimony of My miraculous delivering power. Stay beneath My wings, and I shall make thee as a tower of strength to which the fearful may run and find safety.

# Bread upon the Waters

*Cast thy bread upon the waters:*
*for thou shalt find it after many days.*

ECCLESIASTES 11:1

Ye shall rejoice with exceeding joy, and thy joy shall be shared by angels. Lo, they walk beside thee and guard thy way.

Never limit Me. I will take thee through, though cliffs should rise before thee. There will always be a provision, and in My mercy I shall see that ye find it.

Be humble and be patient. I am nearer to thee than ye think, and will do more than ye expect. I work in every heart to bring conformity to My word. Ye only need give it. I will do the subsequent work. For My Word is Living and Powerful. It shall not come to failure. It shall accomplish My purpose, though My purpose may be entirely hidden from thee.

# The Master Artist

*For we are his workmanship, created
in Christ Jesus unto good works,
which God hath before ordained.*

EPHESIANS 2:10

For I have brought thee through the testing time, and My heart rejoiceth over thee. Thou seest but a part of the picture, but I see the design in its completion. Thou canst not know what is in My mind and what I am creating with the materials of thy life.

Only be thou yielded in My hands. Thou needest not to make thine own plans, for I am in control, and thou wouldst bring disaster by interference, even as a child who would wish to help a master artist, and with untrained use of the brush would ruin the canvas.

So rest thy soul, this knowing, that I have been at work, and in ways thou hast least suspected; for the picture in thy thinking and the work with which I was engaged were entirely different.

# The Master Artist

## PART 2

*For I know the thoughts that I think toward you, saith the LORD, thoughts of peace, and not of evil, to give you an expected end.*

JEREMIAH 29:11

*I make no* idle strokes. What I do is never haphazard. I am never merely mixing colors out of casual curiosity. My every move is one of vital creativity, and every stroke is part of the whole.

Never be dismayed by apparent incongruity. Never be alarmed by a sudden dash of color seemingly out of context. Say only to thy questioning heart, "It is the Infinite wielding His brush; surely He doeth all things well."

And in all that He does with a free hand, without interference, He can stand back and view the work and say, "It is good."

# I Am Bringing Sons into Glory

*And because ye are sons, God hath sent forth the Spirit of his Son into your hearts, crying, Abba, Father.*

GALATIANS 4:6

My people are precious to Me, saith the Lord. No evil shall befall them without My knowledge. My grace have I lavished upon them to conform them to My image. My energies have I given for their nurture and development.

I have not simply brought forth children, but am bringing sons into glory. I have rejoiced in their birth, but rejoice more deeply in their maturity.

Be no more babes, it is written, but GROW. Fed by the Word of God and succored by prayer, let your development into full stature be accomplished.

My hand is upon thee. Draw not back. There may be times when I must wield the rod of correction, but this is for thine ultimate good.

## Shout the Victory

*But thanks be to God, which giveth us the*
*victory through our Lord Jesus Christ.*

1 CORINTHIANS 15:57

My people shall be like an army. They shall move at my command and they shall see the victory. I will not send them into an empty valley. I send them against an on-rushing foe, bent on destruction and armed to the teeth with deadly weapons. They shall overcome them, for I shall be their strength, and I shall make the strength of one to be as the strength of ten. I go before and carry the banner.

Shout the victory. Thy God shall respond. He shall even put to flight the armies of the enemy by the sound of His response.

Peace shall come and shall be as a quiet morning and as the stillness of dew.

# As the Sounding of the Trumpet

*For it is a good thing that the heart
be established with grace.*

HEBREWS 13:9

Be patient, My beloved, for the coming of the Lord is at hand. Establish your hearts in Him, and be ye faithful. The Kingdom is at hand, and shall I not make preparation? Yea, I do not have My prophets simply as demonstrations of the miraculous, I have them for the purpose of communicating My message to My people.

Never has it been more needful that they hear Me. It is as vital at this hour as the contact between an army and their commander. Ye dare not risk being cut off. Ye need direction as never before. Ye also need to know the position and strategy of the opponent. . . . Gird up thy loins. Gather up the supplies. Lay aside every hindrance.

# As the Sounding of the Trumpet
## PART 2

*The house of the wicked shall be overthrown: but the tabernacle of the upright shall flourish.*

PROVERBS 14:11

Surely I am doing a work of righteousness, yea, even in the earth. For I say unto thee, ye are not of the world, even though ye are in the world. I will wash thy feet and cleanse thee from the defilement of the way. I will fit thee to walk in a path of holiness. I will put away false doctrine, and ye shall hear truth. Ye shall eat the good of the land. Ye shall flourish and be made fruitful, saith the Lord.

Because ye have sought Me, I will bless you; yea, I will stand in your midst. I will even joy over thee with singing.

# Ye Shall Come Forth as Gold

*Because thou hast made the Lord,*
*which is my refuge, even the*
*most High, thy habitation.*

PSALM 91:9

Thus saith the Lord, I know the way that ye take, and when thou comest forth, ye shall come forth as gold, yea, as pure gold, having been tried in the fire. For Mine eye is upon thee in loving watchfulness, and Mine ear is open to thy cry.

Be not over-charged with anxiety. I am thy burden-bearer. Be not anxious for the morrow, for on the morrow I shall be thy sure supply. Praise Me NOW, and let thy confidence in Me be manifest. So shall the faith of others be encouraged, for thy life is a witness to many.

The Lord is thy portion: He shall keep thee in peace. Because ye have made the Most High thy abiding place, He shall deliver thee in trouble.

# I Shall Come Singing

*But of that day and that hour knoweth
no man, no, not the angels which are in
heaven, neither the Son, but the Father.
Take ye heed, watch and pray: for ye
know not when the time is.*

MARK 13:32-33

My children, be silent before Me that I may speak to you. I will lift up My voice as the sound of a trumpet—I will speak clearly to you, for the hour is at hand.

Be obedient, and raise thy standards of discipline and dedication to a higher level. For My face is set toward My soon-return to earth. I wait only the release from the Father's hand. Yea, I long to come, and to be united with My chosen ones; but the Father holdeth the times in His own power.

# I Shall Come Singing
## PART 2

*Then brought he me the way of the north gate*
*before the house: and I looked, and, behold,*
*the glory of the LORD filled the house of the*
*LORD: and I fell upon my face.*

EZEKIEL 44:4

And I say unto thee, that though I am ready and longing to come unto thee, yea, would have rejoiced to have come much sooner, lo, I say to thee, thou art not yet ready. I have wooed thee and I have warned thee. Ye have spurned My entreaties, and ye have fought against the restrainings of the spirit.

Break through your religious curtain, and behold Me in My glory. Keep thy vision filled with Me. Keep thy life in tune and thy worship in mutual harmony.

For I shall come singing, and what will ye if ye be in discord?

## Expect the Unexpected

*Teach me to do thy will; for thou art
my God: thy spirit is good; lead me
into the land of uprightness.*

PSALM 143:10

O My child, let Me speak to thee, and let My Spirit direct thy life. I may lead you in unexpected ways, and ask things of you that are startling, but I will never guide you amiss.

Across thy path shall fall the shadow of My hand, and wheresoever I direct thee, there shall ye see My power at work, and there shall come forth from thy ministry that which shall glorify Me.

Do not walk according to thy natural reasonings, but obey the promptings of the Spirit, and be obedient to My voice.

## Expect the Unexpected
### PART 2

*Then Philip went down to the city of Samaria,*
*and preached Christ unto them. And the*
*people with one accord gave heed unto those*
*things which Philip spake, hearing and*
*seeing the miracles which he did.*

ACTS 8:5-6

*I need those* who will be completely flexible in this way, because there are a multitude of souls who are searching for Me, and would never come into contact with Me in a personal way through the channels of the organized church.

Ye shall go as Philip went—at the behest of the Spirit—into the places that are out of the way, and bring light on My Word to those who are in need.

Stay in an attitude of prayer and faith, and I will do all the rest.

# External Destiny of the Present Moment

*And he called his ten servants,*
*and delivered them ten pounds, and*
*said unto them, Occupy till I come.*

LUKE 19:13

O My child, it is not appointed unto thee to know the future, nor to be able to discern aforetime My exact plans. It is enough that we should walk together in love and trust. No doubts need mar thy peace, nor anxieties cloud thy brow. Rest in the knowledge that My ways are perfect and My grace is all-sufficient. Ye shall find My help is adequate, no matter what may befall.

Let none say to thee, "Lo, this shall be, or that shall verily come to pass." Live, rather, in the awareness of the eternal destiny of the present moment. To be unduly occupied with matters of the future is to thine own disadvantage. So much is waiting to be done NOW.

# Scripture Index